T0302252

Design for People Living with Dementia

There were an estimated 50 million people worldwide living with dementia in 2017 and this number will almost double every 20 years, reaching 82 million in 2030. Design has significant potential to contribute to managing this global concern. This book is the first to synthesise the considerable research and projects in dementia and design. Design interactions is a new way of considering how we can improve the relationship between people, products, places and services and of course technology trends, such as the 'internet of things', offer great opportunities in providing new ways to connect people with services and products that can contribute to healthier lifestyles and mechanisms to support people with acute and chronic conditions. In light of this, the book explores the contribution and future potential of design for dementia through the lens of design interactions, such as people, contexts, material and things.

Design for People Living with Dementia is a guide to this innovative and cutting-edge field in healthcare. This book is essential reading for healthcare managers working to provide products, services and care to people with dementia, as well as design researchers and students.

Emmanuel Tsekleves is Senior Lecturer in Design Interactions at Imagination Lancaster, Lancaster University, UK. Emmanuel leads research at the intersection of design, health, well-being and technology. His design-led research attracted media attention by the national press, such as the *Daily Mail*, *Daily Mirror*, *The Times*, *Discovery News* and several other international online media outlets. He blogs regularly for *The Guardian* and *The Conversation* on the design and use of technology in health.

John Keady is Professor of Older Peoples Mental Health, leading the interdisciplinary Dementia and Ageing Research Team at the University of Manchester, UK.

Design for Social Responsibility

Series editor: Rachel Cooper

Social responsibility, in various disguises, has been a recurring theme in design for many years. Since the 1960s several more or less commercial approaches have evolved. In the 1970s designers were encouraged to abandon 'design for profit' in favour of a more compassionate approach inspired by Papanek. In the 1980s and 1990s, profit and ethical issues were no longer considered mutually exclusive and more market-oriented concepts emerged, such as the 'green consumer' and ethical investment. The purchase of socially responsible, 'ethical' products and services has been stimulated by the dissemination of research into sustainability issues in consumer publications. Accessibility and inclusivity have also attracted a great deal of design interest and recently designers have turned to solving social and crime-related problems. Organisations supporting and funding such projects have recently included the NHS (research into design for patient safety); the Home Office has (design against crime); Engineering and Physical Sciences Research Council (design decision-making for urban sustainability).

Businesses are encouraged (and increasingly forced by legislation) to set their own socially responsible agendas that depend on design to be realised. Design decisions all have environmental, social and ethical impacts, so there is a pressing need to provide guidelines for designers and design students within an overarching framework that takes a holistic approach to socially responsible design. This edited series of guides is aimed at students of design, product development, architecture and marketing, and design and management professionals working in the sectors covered by each title. Each volume includes: The background and history of the topic, its significance in social and commercial contexts and trends in the field. Exemplar design case studies. Guidelines for the designer and advice on tools, techniques and resources available.

12. Design for Wellbeing
An Applied Approach
Edited by Ann Petermans and Rebecca Cain

13. Design for Global Challenges and Goals
Edited by Emmanuel Tsekleves, Rachel Cooper and Jak Spencer

14. Design for People Living with Dementia
Interactions and Innovations
Emmanuel Tsekleves and John Keady

For more information about this series, please visit: www.routledge.com/Design-for-Social-Responsibility/book-series/DSR

Design for People Living with Dementia

Interactions and Innovations

Emmanuel Tsekleves and John Keady

Routledge
Taylor & Francis Group

LONDON AND NEW YORK

First published 2021
by Routledge
2 Park Square, Milton Park, Abingdon, Oxon OX14 4RN

and by Routledge
605 Third Avenue, New York, NY 10158

Routledge is an imprint of the Taylor & Francis Group, an informa business

British Library Cataloguing-in-Publication Data
A catalogue record for this book is available from the British Library

Library of Congress Cataloging-in-Publication Data
A catalog record has been requested for this book

ISBN: 978-1-138-33739-8 (hbk)
ISBN: 978-1-032-00017-6 (pbk)
ISBN: 978-0-429-44240-7 (ebk)

Typeset in Times New Roman
by Newgen Publishing UK

Contents

Foreword by series editor

This series began over 15 years ago, its original aim was to raise our awareness and understanding of, not discrete design disciplines such as product or graphic design, but of the contribution of design to social responsibility overall. We began with issues such as overarching themes such as sustainability and inclusivity, but over time the discourse around the wider role of design in terms of contributing more specifically to social, economic and environmental challenges has expanded considerably. We are now aware of the nuanced social challenges that face us globally, dementia is at or near the top of the list.

We are aware of the growth in people living with dementia globally. There will be someone we know who is either living with it, supporting someone with it or delivering a service related to dementia care or prevention. Increasingly in the last ten years, designers have turned their attention not just to designing for an aging population but designing specifically for a dimension of aging. Design for people living with dementia is one of those dimensions and a very important one as Emmanuel Tsekleves and John Keady in this volume will explain.

Although there has been, and is currently, design and design research undertaken in relation to dementia and there are academic papers, yet again we see a field developing without a significant point of reference that defines on the topic, illustrates its antecedents and its current state. This book does just that. Emmanuel and John have worked in the field for several years and are able to provide a lens through which to look at how design contributes to helping people living with dementia, use evidence derived from exemplar case studies but furthermore discuss where the future challenges are and what the potential opportunities for design. As the authors discuss, however, this is not an area purely for design as a discipline and profession. It is a wicked and complex problem that requires design to work alongside all disciplinary perspectives, but also and importantly to engage the perspectives of people who are in some way affected by dementia. They use design interactions as a framework from which to understand the relationship between people, products, places and services and co-design/participatory design as mechanisms for embracing the whole of affected society.

This book provides a baseline from which to build a specialism and offers exciting challenges and models upon which we can move 'design for those living with dementia' forward.

Rachel Cooper
September 2020

Acknowledgements

We would like to thank the following people and personnel without whom none of the text would have been possible:

- All the case study leads in Part 2 of the book who gave us their time and the opportunity to represent their work in this section of the book. You have added to the contents significantly.
- Our Editorial Assistants at Routledge for all your help in getting the book together and in being so supportive behind the scenes.
- Our (anonymous) book proposal reviewers who helped us to shape the direction of the final text.
- Lancaster University and the University of Manchester for allowing us to meet together (in person, online and via email) in order to complete this book together.
- Our respective families.

Emmanuel Tsekleves and John Keady
19 August 2020

Notes on authors

Emmanuel Tsekleves is a senior lecturer in design for health and Associate Director for International research at Imagination Lancaster, Lancaster University, UK.

Driven by the UN's Sustainable Development Goals (SDG), Emmanuel's research focuses on tackling community health challenges across the world. He has lead design research on projects developing health promoting innovations by 'designing out' the problems and barriers that prevent health-promoting behaviours. He conducts cross-disciplinary research by always working (co-designing) with the recipients of health interventions aimed at improving the quality of life and well-being of people into old age, particularly people living with dementia.

Emmanuel is the convenor of the Design Research Society Global Health special interest group, which brings together researchers across disciplines in promoting healthier living. He has made more than 80 academic publications and is the editor of the *Routledge Design for Health* book (2017). Lastly, his research has received extensive public attention in print press and online media outlets, reaching more than 15 million readers in the UK and overseas.

John Keady is a registered mental health nurse and completed his part-time PhD in dementia studies in 1999 using a grounded-theory methodology. Prior to this, he practised for several years as a community psychiatric nurse in dementia care, a position he held in North Wales. Since 2006 John has worked at the Division of Nursing, Midwifery and Social Work, the University of Manchester, UK where he holds a joint position between the University and the Greater Manchester Mental Health NHS Foundation Trust where he is part of the newly-formed Mental Health Nursing Research Unit. John currently leads the interdisciplinary Dementia and Ageing Research Team at The University of Manchester and was the Chief Investigator on the multi-site ESRC/NIHR Neighbourhoods and Dementia Study (2014–2019): https://sites.manchester.ac.uk/neighbourhoods-and-dementia/

John was founding and co-editor of the Sage publications journal '*Dementia: the international journal of social research and practice*' (2002–2018) and is currently a senior fellow at the NIHR School for Social Care Research in the UK. He has written/co-authored a number of peer-reviewed articles and books in dementia care and studies.

1 Introduction

Book need and motivation

The aim of this monograph is to chart the developments of design research in dementia and provide the reader with a cutting-edge and innovative review on this emerging field.

There were an estimated 50 million people worldwide living with dementia in 2017 and this number will almost double every 20 years, reaching 82 million in 2030.[1] Much of the increase will be in developing countries, leading to a considerable impact for millions of families and carers involved in supporting those living with dementia. Dementia is a wicked problem, since cause and effect are often difficult to identify and model, and there is not always consensus on the root problem and solutions (Mitchell et al., 2016). As demonstrated by Tsekleves and Cooper (2017) in their book *Design for Health*, design has the propensity to contribute significantly to complex health-related areas. Furthermore, it identified dementia as a key area in health prevention and healthcare that designers can focus their skills and attention on.

Traditionally designers have paid particular attention to acute and chronic care, through new medical products, hospital, clinic and care home design (Jones, 2013; Tosi et al., 2016). More recently, the complex picture of maintaining population well-being, of health (ill-being) prevention has begun to emerge, and thus the role of designers indirectly in supporting the promotion of healthy lifestyle or in their contribution to ill-being (Cooper et al., 2011).

Design research has now broadened its skill base and its application. Service *design* (Meroni and Sangiorgi, 2011) has introduced a new opportunity to address the improved delivery of products and service both within and outside the healthcare system (Bate and Robert, 2006; Lee, 2011). Behavioural design – grounded in psychology and behaviour change theory – has enabled designer to 'design out' barriers found across objects, services, spaces, environments (Niedderer et al., 2014) and to influence and/or shape human behaviour (Michie et al., 2011). The 'Design in Policy' field is introducing new approaches to developing policy and aiding innovation in organisational, local, regional and national governance (Bason, 2014).

Design interactions is a new way of considering how we can improve the relationship between people, products, places and services and of course technology trends, such as the 'internet of things', offer great opportunities in providing new ways to connect people with services and products that can contribute to healthier lifestyles and mechanisms to support people with acute and chronic conditions. In light of this, the book explores the contribution and future potential of design for dementia through the lens of design interactions, such as people, contexts, material and things.

There is a wide research literature reporting on the psychological and social needs in dementia, from earlier work by Kitwood and Bredin (1992) to more recent reports such as those by Vogt et al. (2012) and McDermott et al. (2019). Much of this literature focuses on designing interventions to support people living with dementia and their caregivers (Span et al., 2013; Rodgers, 2018). For instance, how to facilitate reminiscing to enhance a sense of personhood (Kuwahara et al., 2006; Wallace et al., 2013; Siriaraya and Ang 2014); social interaction and living in the moment (Treadaway and Kenning, 2016; Luján et al., 2017), or to address the safety and autonomy of people living with dementia, to better deal with excessive walking (Lindsay et al., 2012; Holbø et al., 2013); or to support daily living and independence (Mountain, 2006; Ikeda et al., 2011; Ehleringer and Kim 2013; Hoey et al., 2011).

Although there is a considerable amount of design research and projects in dementia, there is no dedicated monograph in this area, which covers the entire spectrum of design and design research that currently exist. Moreover, given the rapid increase of this field, the area of inclusive design does not really cover the nuances of designing for dementia.

In addressing the lacuna of a monograph in this area, the authors have written this book to chart the research projects, methods, challenges and opportunities with the aim of increasing number of researchers engaging in this field.

Book structure and chapter summary

The book is divided into three parts. Part 1 sets the scene by exploring the area of dementia and design research through four lenses employed in design interactions, namely people, contexts, material and things.

More precisely, in Chapter 2, John Keady presents an overview of dementia. Starting with a brief social history of the condition John traces its place and positioning in contemporary society. The chapter then discusses in more detail the different types of dementia and provides information on disease progression and how this affects people living with dementia in their everyday living. The importance of the biopsychosocial model of dementia is highlighted together with the recent addition of a 'physical' domain to open up the intersections between the physical environment and design opportunities. The chapter concludes by setting out recent advancements in citizenship and human rights for people living with dementia.

In Chapter 3, Emmanuel Tsekleves presents the challenges for design across the different facets of our society. The chapter addresses challenges related to diagnosis, care, quality of life, research and ethics as well as the different contexts where research in dementia is targeted, such as the home, nursing home, hospital and community. Through analysis of the relevant literature, it provides researchers, especially those who employ design research methods, with a better understanding of the challenges people living with dementia, as well as their family and caregivers face. Opportunities where design research can intervene and support people living with dementia are highlighted and discussed too.

Chapter 4, by John Keady, provides the reader with an understanding about the different design research methods that can actively be used to both support and empower people living with dementia. Adhering to the underpinning vision and values of this book, the chapter outlines participatory approaches to research and the importance of co-design and co-production alongside people living with dementia. It covers patient and public involvement in research and offers a discussion on how people living with dementia might want to be positioned in the research process, from setting the research question to taking part in dissemination activities. It introduces the COINED model that focuses towards a more egalitarian and democratised approach to undertaking and evaluating design research. The chapter concludes with two brief examples of relevant work where design research methods have been used and applied in the dementia studies field.

The last chapter in Part 1, Chapter 5, by Emmanuel Tsekleves, provides an overview of design research work that contributes to the context of dementia through the research, design and development of relevant non-pharmacological interventions. In doing so it maps the landscape of design research in this field, outlining several opportunities for design researchers in this field. Drawing from the literature, the chapter identifies four key research themes where design research effort has recently been focused, namely: (i) reminiscence and personhood, (ii) social interaction and living in the moment, (iii) independent and assisted living and (iv) cognitive and physical stimulation.

Part 2 presents in more detail ten case studies across different research contexts in designing for people living with dementia. The case studies are representative of current work in the area and have been drawn from an international pool of research projects. The case studies are based on synthesising published work and material, such as on outward facing websites, supplemented by either face-to-face or online video interviews with the identified project researchers.

Case study 1 presents a UK-based research project that explored reminiscence and personhood (focusing on regeneration and about how community and neighbourhoods had changed) through a participatory research approach with people living with dementia and their caregivers.

Case study 2 provides an overview of the MinD project, designing for people with dementia: designing for mindful self-empowerment and social engagement. The project took place across different European countries exploring social interaction and personhood via participatory design methods.

Case study 3 focuses on independent and assisted living, employing user-centred design to explore and re-design hygiene overalls for people living with dementia in care homes in Finland.

Case study 4 presents a project in Melbourne, Australia that explores the role music and technology can play in social interactions for people living with dementia. The music ensemble project employed participatory design.

Case study 5 explores how design can connect a group of people living with dementia in a care facility in Netherlands, through the user-centred design of leisure products that enhance reminiscence and personhood.

Case study 6 presents the design a home for people living with dementia that aims to support ageing-in-place that could be used as a demonstration dwelling for training and education in Netherlands.

Case study 7 describes a project that designed and developed an interactive and networked music system for people living with dementia in Germany, focusing on enhancing reminiscence and personhood via participatory design.

Case study 8 presents the LAUGH (Ludic Artefacts Using Gesture and Haptics) research project, which worked alongside people living with late-stage dementia to design playful products whose function was to support 'in the moment' living and personhood.

Case study 9 describes a social and recreational day programme for people living with young onset dementia in Vancouver, Canada, focusing on design innovation through observation and ethnographic research methods.

Case study 10 explores the use of setting up and undertaking case study research with people living with dementia attending a series of improvised music-making sessions in the North West of the UK.

Part 3 of the book consists of one chapter and provides a foresight into the research in dementia by identifying the opportunities and emerging trends for researchers. This final chapter in the book, Chapter 6, explores beyond the state-of-the-art that arise from the literature as well as the interviews conducted with ten international experts in the development of the case studies, presented in Part 2 of the book. It discusses in more detail five emergent themes where design research can make a significant contribution in the dementia studies field. These five themes are: (i) people living with dementia as co-researchers, (ii) design for agency and daily living, (iii) evidence-based design and co-design, (iv) researcher training on people living with dementia and (v) emerging and unexplored research areas. This fifth theme embraces the prospect and opportunities involved in conducting design research studies in Global South countries, focusing on dementia prevention and dementia and gender.

We hope that you enjoy the book and it gives as much pleasure as we have had in writing it.

Note

1 www.alz.co.uk/research/statistics.

References

Bason, C. (2014). *Design for Policy. Design for Social Responsibility Series*. London: Routledge.

Bate, P. and Robert, G. (2006). Experience-based design: from redesigning the system around the patient to co-designing services with the patient. *Quality and Safety in Health Care*, 15 (5): 307–310.

Cooper, R. and Boyko, C. (2011). Design for health: the relationship between design and non- communicable diseases. *Journal of Health Communication*, 16: 134–157.

Ehleringer, E. H. and Kim, S. J. (2013). "The Wearable Lullaby: Improving Sleep Quality of Caregivers of Dementia Patients." In *CHI'13 Extended Abstracts on Human Factors in Computing Systems*, pp. 409–414. New York: ACM.

Hoey, J., Ploetz, T., Jackson, D., Monk, A., Pham, C. and Olivier, P. (2011). "Rapid specification and automated generation of prompting systems to assist people with dementia." *Pervasive and Mobile Computing*, 7 (3): 299–318.

Holbø, K., Bøthun, S. and Dahl, Y. (2013, October). "Safe Walking Technology for People with Dementia: What Do They Want?" In *Proceedings of the 15th International ACM SIGACCESS Conference on Computers and Accessibility*, p. 21. New York: ACM.

Ikeda, S., Asghar, Z., Hyry, J., Pulli, P., Pitkanen, A. and Kato, H. (2011). "Remote Assistance Using Visual Prompts for Demented Elderly in Cooking." In *Proceedings of the 4th International Symposium on Applied Sciences in Biomedical and Communication Technologies*. pp. 1–5. New York: ACM.

Jones, P. J. (2013). *Design for Care: Innovating Healthcare Experience*. New York: Rosenfeld.

Kitwood, T. and Bredin, K. (1992). Towards a theory of dementia care: personhood and well-being. *Ageing & Society*, 12 (3): 269–287.

Kuwahara, N., Abe, S., Yasuda, K. and Kuwabara, K. (2006). "Networked Reminiscence Therapy for Individuals with Dementia by Using Photo and Video Sharing." In *Proceedings of the 8th International ACM SIGACCESS Conference on Computers and Accessibility*, pp. 125–132. New York: ACM.

Lee, S. (2011). Evaluating serviceability of healthcare servicescapes: service design perspective. *International Journal of Design*, 5(2): 521–530.

Lindsay, S., Brittain, K., Jackson, D., Ladha, C., Ladha, K. and Olivier, P. (2012). "Empathy, Participa- tory Design and People with Dementia." In *Proceedings of the SIGCHI Conference on Human Factors in Computing Systems*, pp. 521–530. New York: ACM.

Luján Escalante, M., Tsekleves, E., Bingley, A. F. and Gradinar, A. (2017). 'Ageing Playfully': a story of forgetting and remembering. *Design for Health*, 1(1): 134–145

McDermott, O., Charlesworth, G., Hogervorst, E., Stoner, C., Moniz-Cook, E., Spector, A., Csipke, E. and Orrell, M. (2019). Psychosocial interventions for people with dementia: a synthesis of systematic reviews. *Aging & Mental Health*, 23 (4): 393–403.

Meroni, A. and Sangiorgi, D. (2011). *Design for Services. Design for Social Responsibility Series*. London: Gower Publishing.

Michie, S., van Stralen, M. M. and West, R. (2011). The behaviour change wheel: a new method for characterising and designing behaviour change interventions. *Implementation Science*, 6 (1): 42.

Mitchell, J. I., Long, J. C., Braithwaite, J. and Brodaty, H. (2016). Social-professional networks in long-term care settings with people with dementia: an approach to better care? A systematic review. *Journal of the American Medical Directors Association*, 17 (2): 17–27.

Mountain, G. A. (2006). Self-management for people with early dementia: an exploration of concepts and supporting evidence. *Dementia*, 5 (3): 429–446.

Niedderer, K., Mackrill, J., Clune, S., Lockton, D., Ludden, G., Morris, A., Cain, R., Gardiner, E., Gutteridge, R., Evans, M. and Hekkert, P. (2014). *Creating Sustainable Innovation through Design for Behaviour Change: Summary Report.* Wolverhampton: University of Wolverhampton, CADRE.

Rodgers, P. A. (2018.) Co-designing with people living with dementia. *CoDesign*, 14 (3): 188–202.

Siriaraya, P. and Ang, C. S. (2014). "Recreating Living Experiences from Past Memories Through Virtual Worlds for People with Dementia." In *Proceedings of the SIGCHI Conference on Human Factors in Computing Systems*, pp. 3977–3986. New York, NY: ACM.

Span, M., Hettinga, M., Vernooij-Dassen, M., Eefsting, J. and Smits, C. (2013). Involving people with dementia in the development of supportive IT applications: a systematic review. *Ageing Research Reviews*, 12 (2): 535–551.

Tosi, F., Rinaldi, A. and Ricci, D. B. (2016). "Ergonomics and Inclusive Design: Innovative Medical Devices for Home Care." In Di Bucchianico, G. (ed) *Advances in Design for Inclusion*, pp. 401–412.Washington: Springer.

Treadaway, C. and Kenning, G. (2016). Sensor e-textiles: person centered co-design for people with late stage dementia. *Working with Older People*, 20 (2): 76–85.

Tsekleves, E. and Cooper, R. (Eds.). (2017). *Design for Health. Design for Social Responsibility*. London: Routledge.

Vogt, J., Luyten, K., Van den Bergh, J., Coninx, K. and Meier, A. (2012). Putting dementia into context. *Human-Centered Software Engineering*, pp. 181–198. Berlin, Heidelberg: Springer.

Wallace, J., Wright, P. C., McCarthy, J., Green, D. P., Thomas, J. and Olivier, P. (2013). "A Design-Led Inquiry into Personhood in Dementia." In *Proceedings of the SIGCHI Conference on Human Factors in Computing Systems*, pp. 2617–2626. New York: ACM.

Part 1

Design for people living with dementia in context

2 People

An overview of dementia

A brief history of dementia

It is important to recognise that 'dementia' – however it is defined/
constructed – is not a new phenomenon and in all likelihood has been part
of the human experience from our earliest times. As an illustration, in the
hieroglyphics of the *Maxims of the Ptah Holy* from the 9th century BC, Loza
and Milad (1990) found the following translated account of the experience of
old age in Ancient Egypt:

> My Sovereign master, old age, is here. Senility has descended on me; the
> weakness of my childhood has returned. My eyes are weak, my ears are
> deaf, my nose is blocked and can no longer breathe. My taste is com-
> pletely gone. My spirit forgetful and I can no longer remember yesterday.
> What was nice has become bad. What causes senility in men is bad in
> every way.
>
> (p. 403, slightly abridged)

From a sociological and historical standpoint, what is interesting in this
statement is not only the recognisable and enduring negative stereotypes
associated with the ageing process, but also that recent forgetfulness and
memory loss were clearly associated with advancing age, criterion that endures
to the present in the establishment of a diagnosis of dementia (American
Psychiatric Association, 2013).

Moving forward two millennium and changing the landscape from the
desert sands of ancient Egypt to the green and rolling countryside of medieval England, Neugebauer (1978, cited in Brayne and Calloway, 1990, p. 310),
whilst undertaking historical sociological research, uncovered a battery of
questions that were used in 1383 to assess Emma de Beston for Cambridge
for 'idiocy':

- In what town she was in
- How many husbands she had had
- How many days there were in a week

- How many shillings there were in 40 pence
- If she would rather have 20 silver groats than 40 pence

Arguably, these questions provide the basis for an initial screen of Emma de Beston's abilities at problem-solving, orientation and memory which is specifically cued into her autobiographical memory, i.e. how many husbands she had had. Whilst language and social norms/values change over time and between cultures, arguable the battery of questions from medieval England is not dissimilar in scope to many of today's brief cognitive screening/assessment tools to test for the onset of dementia/memory problems conducted in primary care. We will return to the recognition and diagnosis of dementia once again a little later in the chapter.

However, remaining in the historical past and in the UK, for people with a mental illness the end of the 18th century and the beginning of the 19th century were times of great social change as the episodic periods of insanity exhibited by King George III (1782–1820) challenged the population to look more sympathetically at such issues. Indeed, as described by Skultans (1979, pp. 10–11), the King's plight forced Parliament to set up a committee to review his 'insanity' and plan how help could best be provided – this resulted in two reports published in 1807 and 1815. More importantly, and reflecting the public mood of the time, in 1806 Parliament passed an Act recommending that each county build an asylum for the care of its insane. This change of social attitudes towards 'the insane', which included people living with dementia (see: Berrios, 1987), coincided with Pinel's (1787) pioneering research into 'brain disease' and his classification of 'demence' to define a cluster of signs that involved a lack of judgement, disconnected ideas and lost faculty of mental attention.

By the early part of the 19th century 'dementia' – the English translation of 'demence' – was brought into medical discourse and practice to describe 'any state of psychological dysfunction associated with chronic brain disease' (Goldberg et al., 1988, p. 188). Given this description, 'dementia' could be applied to any age group and hence the use of the term 'dementia praecox' became associated with the signs and symptoms of what we would recognise today as schizophrenia in younger adults (Goldberg et al., 1988). However, it was not until the latter parts of the 19th century that a more contemporary context for the understanding of dementia can be found. Whilst undertaking anatomical dissection of 'a diseased brain', Marcé (1863) reported the existence of cortical atrophy, enlarged ventricles and tissue softening and suggested that this was the macroscopic hallmark of 'senile dementia'. Further, Binswanger (1898, cited in Allison, 1962, p. 10) first coined the term 'presenile dementia' with 'presenile' being used to refer to symptoms developing in a person between forty and sixty years of age and 'dementia' to imply impairment of memory and intellect. Accordingly, the initial focus of neurological research into the syndrome of 'dementia' was concerned with the link between younger, middle-aged, people with impaired memory and intellect and the as yet unknown role played by atheroma and arteriosclerosis in this process. Arnold Pick's writings between 1892 and 1908 exemplify this point when he described a rare and particular presenile 'cortical atrophy' in the frontal and temporal lobes of the brain – the reported syndrome (Pick's disease) continues to bear his name to this day. Such advancements in clinical identification were aided immeasurably in the mid-1880s by improvements in scientific equipment, particularly microscopes.

Citing Pick's work in Prague as a prime example, Berrios (1990) reports that the clinical descriptions of dementia started 'in earnest' during this period. Changes in brain pathology were singled out as important, such as cellular death and disintegration, and the existence of plaques and neurofibrils; however, the link between these processes was as yet unknown. Thus by the early 1900s, efforts were being made to measure the symptoms and severity of dementia, ascertain the differential importance of senile and vascular aetiology of dementia and study the comparative prevalence of senile dementia in relation to other psychiatric conditions affecting older people. These enquiries were directly influenced by Marinesco (1900) whose theories on the ageing of brain tissue prompted Alois Alzheimer to explore brain pathology. It is at this junction in time that medical history and discovery intersect to drive forward our present-day understandings of Alzheimer's disease and its positioning with the ranges of dementias.

Staying with the background and work of Alois Alzheimer for now, during his formative years Alzheimer studied medicine in Berlin, Tübigen and Würzburg before he joined Franz Nissl in 1888 at the psychiatric hospital in Frankfurt, Germany. Franz Nissl convinced Alzheimer that he should investigate the cerebral cortex in mental disorders and apply Nissl's recently developed 'staining techniques' to the identification of nerve cells in the brain – a procedure through which the first reliable morphological assessment of nerve cells became possible. Indeed, it was Alzheimer (1897) who was to publish the first neurohistological study of schizophrenia, a feat he achieved before moving to Munich in 1903 to work with Emille Kraeplin. Here, Alzheimer took up the joint post of Assistant Clinical Director of the Frankfurt am Main insane asylum and Director of the Anatomical Laboratory. It was in this position that Alzheimer conducted his seminal neurological and observational research on cognitive functioning and memory decline on the (at the time) 52-year old Auguste Deter (who was to die in 1906 at the age of 56 in the asylum), eventually publishing his most influential paper 'Über eine eigenartige Erkankung der Hirnrinde', literally translated as 'Munich: On an Unusual Illness of the Cerebral Cortex' (Alzheimer, 1907). This paper on the study of Auguste Deter's deceased and atrophied brain was to change the course of medical and social understanding of dementia and consolidate the medical dominance of dementia for much of the remainder of the 20th century. Arguably this medical dominance continues into the first part of the 21st century as witnessed by the current £290m investment in the UK Dementia Research Institute (UK DRI) to search for a cure to Alzheimer's disease and to fulfil the ambition identified in Prime Minister's 2020 Challenge on Dementia (Department of Health, 2015; and see: https://ukdri.ac.uk/; accessed 7 June 2020). Uncovering the biology of Alzheimer's disease and other dementias remains highly influential, although it is not the only story in the dementia-studies narrative.

Defining and refining dementia

Moving to the present day, dementia is a general term that covers a wide range of neurocognitive changes and their associated symptoms which, in turn, characterise a number of variable conditions. In the most recent edition of the American Psychiatric Association's Diagnostic and Statistical Manual of Mental Disorders (DSM-5; American Psychiatric Association, 2013), dementia is defined as a major neurocognitive disorder. The DSM-5 also identifies earlier stages of cognitive decline in a new diagnostic category of mild neurocognitive disorder. Perhaps more importantly, the DSM-5 acknowledges that the term 'dementia' is still in common usage and therefore remains appropriate for describing the various subtypes of dementia – an acknowledgement that we will use both during this chapter and throughout the book. Accordingly, the terminology of 'dementia' will be used to describe a range of cognitive and behavioural symptoms that can include memory loss, problems with reasoning and communication and change in personality and a reduction in a person's ability to carry out daily activities, such as shopping, washing, dressing and cooking.

As indicated by the Alzheimer's Society (2019b), there are over 100 different types of dementia with the most common being:

- Alzheimer's disease (62% of cases)
- Vascular dementia (17% of cases)
- Mixed dementia (10% of cases; this is where a person is believed to have a combination of two or more kinds of dementia. The term is most commonly used when Alzheimer's disease and Vascular dementia coexist)

The less common forms of dementia include corticobasal degeneration, Creutzfeldt-Jakob disease and Huntington's disease. Other than in rare instances, such as early identification and diagnosis of alcohol-related brain damage, there are no cures for any of the dementias. Therefore, knowing what type of dementia someone has is important for providing information to the person and their family/support network and in planning care and support for all involved.

Dementia is also seen as a progressive condition, which means that the symptoms will gradually get worse. This progression will vary from person to person and each person will experience their diagnosis of dementia differently. Similarly, people living with dementia may often have some of the same general symptoms, but the degree to which these affect each person will vary. In the DSM-5 classification, mild and major forms of all subtypes of dementia (such as Alzheimer's disease) have been assigned diagnostic criteria. While varying in pathology and presentation, all of these subtypes in both mild and major form are characterised by impacts upon six key cognitive domains, namely:

1. Complex attention, such as selective attention and speed of information processing
2. Executive function, such as decision-making and working memory
3. Learning and memory, such as recognition memory, semantic and auto-biographical long-term memory
4. Language, such as object naming, word finding, fluency, grammar and syntax
5. Perceptual-motor function, such as visual perception and perceptualmotor coordination
6. Social cognition, such as recognition of emotions

The DSM-5 classification further attributes sub-domains to each of these six cognitive domains and interested readers are advised to see the source reference as a continued explanation and discussion falls outside of the remit for this chapter (see: American Psychiatric Association, 2013).

Reaching a diagnosis of dementia

An early and timely diagnosis of dementia is a world-wide policy and practice imperative (Alzheimer's Disease International, 2011). In the UK, guidance for helping clinicians to make a diagnosis of dementia is included in the most recent National Institute for Health and Care Excellence (NICE) dementia guideline (NICE, 2018). Here, it is acknowledged that a diagnosis can be reached for a person with suspected dementia in a non-specialist setting, such as by a general practitioner in primary care. The key tasks in an initial assessment of suspected dementia is to:

- Take a history from the person with suspected dementia him- or herself and if possible, from someone who knows the person well (such as a family member)
- Focus on cognitive, behavioural and psychological symptoms
- Measure the impact that such symptoms have on the person's daily life
- Undertake a physical examination and take appropriate blood and urine tests to exclude reversible causes of cognitive decline
- Use cognitive testing, such as the 6-item cognitive impairment test (6-CIT; for a discussion on the 6-CIT instrument and issues of validity and reliability see: O'Sullivan et al., 2016)

Alternatively, a person with suspected dementia can be referred to a specialist dementia diagnostic service, such as a memory clinic or community old-age psychiatry service, in certain circumstances. In the NICE (2018) dementia guideline two main circumstances are outlined where this specialist referral is indicated. Firstly, if reversible causes of cognitive decline are suspected, such as delirium, depression and sensory impairment (e.g. sight or hearing loss). Secondly, if cognitive impairment from medicines associated with increased anticholinergic burden have been investigated but dementia is still suspected.

Reaching an early diagnosis of dementia enables the person living with the condition to come to terms with its onset and course and allows life adjustments to be made at a pace and timing that is best suited to the individual and their social networks (Samsi et al., 2014). For some people living with dementia, such support will mean attending a support group and/or getting involved in a self-advocacy group to push for change and increased social awareness. Whilst for others, an early diagnosis will mean more time to adjust to the diagnosis and to prepare for the future which will include changing relational and social circumstances, including planning for future care needs. There is no one way to successfully 'live well' with dementia following a diagnosis, but choices and supporting the person living with dementia to make their own decisions for as long as is possible will help to 'normalise' events and keep the person connected to their lives and to their meaningful relationships.

The prevalence of dementia

The classification and identification of the type(s) of dementia is important as dementia currently affects approximately over 46.8 million people around the world (Alzheimer's Disease International, 2015), with this number set to rise as the world's population increases and ages. According to the Alzheimer's Society (2014), in the UK there are approximately 850,000 people living with dementia, 700,000 of whom live in England. Moreover, in the UK, there are 42,000 people living with dementia under the age of 65 and an estimated 25,000 people from black, Asian and minority ethnic communities. The numbers of people living with dementia in the UK will increase to over 1.6 million by 2040. Importantly, the same report (Alzheimer's Society, 2019a) identifies that the risk developing dementia increases exponentially with age, rising from 1 in 14 over the age of 65 to 1 in 6 over the age 80. Another way of viewing this prevalence rate is to say that the probability of developing dementia almost doubles every five years after the age of 65. In the UK almost two-thirds of people living with dementia live in their own homes with up to 90% of care provided by family and/or friends. The remaining one-third live in supported accommodation, such as in a care home or in extra-care housing (Alzheimer's Society, 2019a).

Furthermore, at any one time, up to 25% of general hospital beds are occupied by people living with dementia and more than 97% of general hospital staff report having cared for patients living with dementia (Alzheimer's

Society, 2014). However, these hospital-based numbers will fluctuate following the declared world pandemic caused by the coronavirus COVID-19 (March 2020 onwards) and additional figures and research will be needed going forward (Department of Health and Social Care, 2020). It is also important to recognise that more women than men live with dementia and that women are more likely to take on a caregiving role in the home and in supported accommodation, e.g. care home practice (Erol et al., 2016). Around seven in ten people who live with a dementia also live with at least one other medical condition, such as chronic obstructive pulmonary disease or heart disease (All-Party Parliamentary Group on Dementia, 2016). This is significant as any design interventions for people living with dementia will, in all likelihood, have to take into account other conditions and/or restricted physical mobility as well as the 'stage' of dementia that the person is living through, as we will now outline.

The stages of dementia

Numerous clinical and policy reports discuss the importance and value of recognising the stages of the dementia and what stage the person with the diagnosis of dementia is living through (see for example: Alzheimer's Society, 2015; NICE, 2018). These stages are normally presented as either a three or a seven-stage model and start with a transition from a person's healthy status into one where the person experiences the first signs and symptoms of dementia. Whilst the language and definitions in the models may differ, what unifies the stages is that over time change – based on an accumulative deficit model – will gradually happen to a person living with a diagnosis of dementia and that the person's death is included in the final stage of each model.

For the three-stage model of dementia, this is seen to transition through a mild (or early) stage into a moderate (or middle) stage and then onto a severe (or late) stage (Alzheimer's Society, 2015). It is in the severe (or late) stage of the journey through dementia that the person's death will occur should the person not die of other causes in between times. Based on the work of Molli Grossman (see: www.kindlycare.com/stages-of-dementia/; accessed 7 June 2020) we will now delineate and develop these three stages of dementia a little more and attune this attention to Alzheimer's disease as this is the most prevalent sub-type of dementia.

Mild (or early) stage

In the mild stage of Alzheimer's disease, symptoms typically include forgetfulness, losing or misplacing things, difficulty finding the right words and showing poor judgment with planning and decision-making. People with mild Alzheimer's disease might be unable able to recall a recent conversation or the name of a familiar object, even though it might be on the tip of their tongue.

Moderate (or middle) stage

In this stage, people with Alzheimer's disease are more likely to experience increased confusion, greater memory loss and worsening judgment. They may also exhibit confusion about orientation, such as where they are or what day it is, and have difficulty recalling personal information, such as their address or telephone number or important dates like birthdays or anniversaries. During this time, people with moderate dementia may get lost when outside and become unable to successfully wayfind even though the environment, or route, may have been familiar to the person for many years. In the moderate stage, people living with Alzheimer's disease are likely to begin to need more help in their everyday lives, especially with their activities of daily living such as dressing, bathing and grooming. Sleep patterns may also become irregular and the person may start to experience behaviours that challenge, such as restlessness, excessive walking, hitting, screaming, apathy, sexual inappropriateness, shouting, agitation and violent and aggressive resistance towards help with personal care. It is also important to recognise that a person living with Alzheimer's disease, and other forms of dementia of course, can experience more than one of the behaviours that challenge at the same time. This presentation of non-cognitive symptoms is known by different names such as 'challenging behaviour', 'neuropsychiatric symptoms' and 'behavioural and psychological symptoms of dementia', also known as BPSDs (NICE, 2018).

Around 90% of all people living with dementia will experience behaviours that challenge at some point during their diagnosis, but it is more likely to be at this stage and transitioning into the severe (or late) stage (Moniz-Cook et al., 2017). Family carers can often misinterpret and misunderstand changes in a person living with dementia's behaviour and see it as 'antisocial' rather than as a part of the overall presentation of dementia. Education is an important part of any formulation and intervention plan, such as that contained in the Newcastle Challenging Behaviour model (James and Jackman, 2017). Behaviours that challenge are recognised as a major component of the syndrome of dementia and in need of skilled identification and intervention. They are also recognised as a major stressor for family carers and a reason why people living with dementia enter supported living accommodation such as a care home (Keady and Jones, 2010).

Severe (or late) stage

In the severe stage of Alzheimer's disease, there is a marked decline in physical functioning which begins to mirror the decline in the person's cognitive functioning. During this stage, individuals with Alzheimer's typically lose their ability to communicate fluently or engage in conversation, although they may still be able to speak. Alongside these changes, individuals typically begin to experience a loss of their physical capabilities, including difficulty eating and swallowing, an inability to control bladder and bowel movements and a

difficulty walking that eventually results in an inability to walk. In all likelihood, people with severe Alzheimer's disease will require full-time assistance
and the person has an increased susceptibility to infections, such as pneu-
monia, which is a common cause of death in individuals with dementia.

In contrast to this three-stage model, Reisberg et al. (1988) outlined a
seven-stage model of Alzheimer's disease which is more commonly referred
to as the Global Deterioration Scale (GDS). Whilst the language is a little
out of date to contemporary thinking, the GDS remains in common usage
in clinical practice and we have therefore summarised its key elements below:

Stage 1:   No impairment – no memory loss
Stage 2:   Very mild cognitive decline – normal memory loss associated
           with aging
Stage 3:   Mild cognitive decline – friends and family members begin to
           notice cognitive problems
Stage 4:   Moderate cognitive decline – neurologists can confidently
           diagnose Alzheimers; poor short-term memory, may forget personal
           details, difficulty with simple arithmetic calculations
Stage 5:   Moderately severe cognitive decline – the person begins to need
           help with daily activities, significant confusion, disorientation, may
           no longer be possible to live alone
Stage 6:   Severe cognitive decline – worsened memory loss, difficulty
           recognising family members, some personality changes
Stage 7:   Very severe cognitive decline – final stage; communication is
           limited, physical systems also decline

Whilst it is not possible to put a time frame around how long a person living
with dementia will spend in one stage, or how long it may take to transition
through all three (or seven) stages, it is known that a diagnosis of dementia
is associated with a reduction in median life expectancy. For example, in a
comprehensive study by Wolters et al. (2019), this reduction was established
at close to 60% (53% for women and 63% for men) when dementia was
diagnosed between the ages of 65 and 69 and about 20% (24% for women
and 21% for men) when diagnosed between the ages 85 and 89 years. It is
also well-known that people with rarer and/or younger onset dementia have a
significant shorter life expectancy than the general population who are living
without dementia at the same age (see: Gerritsen, 2019).

Dementia and the biopsychosocial model

The biopsychosocial model of health was first introduced in the mid-1970s
by the American psychiatrist George Engel who argued that the traditional
medical model was fundamentally limited in its scope and ability to provide
practitioners with the rounded evidence-base necessary for clinical decision-
making (Engel, 1977). Instead, Engel put forward the idea that health was

better viewed through interconnected systems of biological (focus on disease), psychological (thoughts, emotions, feelings with a focus on psychological testing and measurement) and sociological (the person's social context) spectrums and that the 'disruptive effects of (psychiatric) illness' are an interplay within and between these fields (Engel, 1977). It was a persuasive argument as issues of (psychiatric) presentation, diagnosis, treatment and follow up could now be attributed to a biopsychosocial approach with the model serving to explain a multitude of phenomena that immediately brought a more inclusive and multidisciplinary agenda to psychiatry and psychiatric practice (Engel, 1980).

As a heuristic device, the biopsychosocial model continues to be used and aligned to areas of contemporary psychiatry (for a discussion see: Ghaemi, 2010) although it has branched out from its psychiatric roots and found an adoptive home in other areas of clinical practice and sociological understandings. Indeed, Borrell-Carrió et al. (2004) have also suggested that due to its extensive use and application, the biopsychosocial model has morphed away from its systems routes and into a philosophy of care that neatly fits with the lexicon and narrative of clinical practice – an issue in dementia care that has been commented on by both Sabat (2011) and Revolta et al. (2016). In other words, to undertake a biopsychosocial approach to practice is, de facto, to deliver holistic, evidence-based care. The biopsychosocial model has also been applied to dementia as an approach to ground practice, clinical understanding and evidence-based decision-making, such as expressed in the UK through the first National Institute for Health and Clinical Excellence (NICE) and the Social Care Institute for Excellence (SCIE) Dementia guideline (NICE/SCIE, 2006).

As an illustration of its utility, Sabat (2008), when outlining the biopsychosocial approach to dementia, aligned it in the following way:

- The biological domain to the depletion of certain transmitter substances within the human brain and the impact that this has for the person's memory functioning and cognitive abilities, including visual identification of objects due to damage to the occipital lobe.
- The psychological domain to an opportunity to engage with the person living with dementia as a person first and foremost whose behaviour is driven by the meaning that situations hold for him or her (i.e. as a 'semiotic subject'; see also Sabat and Harré, 1994).
- The social domain to the importance of the person living with dementia having a valued social identity, one where language is used positively to socially position the person as someone of intrinsic worth and value.

Countering the dominance of the biological understanding of dementia in the latter part of the 20th century was significant and in teasing out the psychological and social components of dementia. Prime amongst this shift in conceptualisation was work in the UK led by Dr (later Professor) Tom

Kitwood and his colleagues at the Bradford Dementia Group. This work started towards the end of the 1980s and Kitwood and the team developed an elegant social theory of personhood in dementia which, in time, went on to influence UK public and health policy and have global impact.

True to the philosophy of a person-centred approach, this social theory did not emerge from the consideration of data collected from a large numbers of individuals. It was, instead, built around a single case history, or psychobiography as it was originally named, undertaken by Kitwood himself (Kitwood, 1990a). This psychobiography was conducted by Kitwood in the late 1980s with a person called 'Rose' whose struggle to assert her personality through the mask of her confusion triggered Kitwood's thoughts on the need to reconceptualise the experience of dementia. After attempting to agree a meaning to Rose's actions and behaviours with colleagues at the Bradford Dementia Group (see: Kitwood, 1990a for a fuller discussion), the team constructed a multi-dimensional theory that identified a range of social and subjective factors that they believed shaped Rose's experiences. Whilst the emerging theory focused predominantly on the later stages of dementia in residential care, mirroring Rose's personal circumstances at the time, it nevertheless placed the person with dementia at the heart of the formulation. It was from these observations that Kitwood (1988) used an equation to reconceptualise the experience of living with dementia along the following lines:

$$SD = P + B + H + NI + SP$$

In this equation SD refers to senile dementia which is viewed as the product of the complex interactions between the remaining five elements of the equation:

P = Personality, which includes coping styles and defences against anxiety
B = Biography, and responses to the vicissitudes of later life
H = Health status, including the acuity of the senses
NI = Neurological impairment, separated into its location, type and intensity
SP = Social psychology which constitutes the fabric of everyday life

Kitwood (1988) suggested that the equation accounted for most of the phenomenon associated with the range of dementias and explained the unique course of each person's dementia by combining 'structural' and 'conjunctural' means of explanation. This theory reflected Kitwood's (1990b, 1997) critique of the past failings of care environments and approaches to people living with dementia which, for Kitwood (1990b), created a 'malignant social psychology' that inhibited the full expression and selfhood of people living with dementia. Crucial to the emerging theory was the acceptance of the construct of 'personhood' and the recognition that a 'malignant social psychology' had been developed which 'bore down powerfully' on those living with dementia (Kitwood and Bredin, 1992a). Kitwood (1990b) initially outlined 10 components that illustrated the elements of this 'malignant social psychology' but later extended these to 17 by the time of the publication of the now seminal text 'Dementia reconsidered: the person comes first' (Kitwood, 1997, pp. 46–47). Examples of the factors that Kitwood believed created a 'malignant social psychology' included:

> Infantilization: implying that a dementia sufferer has the mentality or capability of a baby or young child;
> Stigmatization: turning a person living with dementia into an alien, a diseased object, an outcast, especially through verbal labels;
> Outpacing: delivering information or instruction at a rate far beyond what can be processed;
> Objectification: treating a person like a lump of dead matter; to be measured, pushed around, drained, filled and so on;
> Ignoring: carrying on (in conversation or action) in the presence of a person as if they were not there.

Kitwood and his colleagues cogently argued that the 'dementia' is not the main problem, rather it is 'our' (individual, carer, professional, society) inability to accommodate 'their' view of the world into everyday frames of reference. Kitwood and Bredin (1992a) suggested that this 'them' and 'us' divide creates a dialectic tension that is reinforced over the years by the devalued status of someone who is labelled as 'demented' and who is consequently seen to be cognitively incompetent (see also: Sabat et al., 2011). Underpinning these observations is the belief that if the elements of a 'malignant social psychology' can be identified, appraised and overcome, then care (both for family and professional carers) can be improved and that the person with dementia will achieve a greater sense of personal 'well-being'. This focus on well-being is reflected in Kitwood's (1997) well-known definition of personhood, namely:

> It is a standing or status that is bestowed upon one human being, by others, in the context of relationship and social being. It implies recognition, respect and trust. Both the according of personhood, and the failure to do so, have consequences that are empirically testable.
>
> (p. 8)

To promote the practice of person-centred care the observational method of Dementia Care Mapping (Kitwood, 1990b; Kitwood and Bredin, 1992b) was devised with the goal of not only enhancing care in formal settings, but of capturing it in a measurable way. Kitwood and Bredin (1992a) argued that a positive change to the social environment could cause a reversal of the accepted 'decline' trajectory in dementia (i.e. from mild to moderate to late stages) and named this 'rementia'. Moreover, promoting the importance of maintaining personhood throughout the progression of dementia was seen to occur by meeting psychosocial needs such as attachment, inclusion, comfort, identity, occupation and love (Kitwood, 1997, p. 82).

Such a paradigm shift had implications for the caring professions as people living with dementia were now seen to exert a sense of agency, an agency that could only be realised through significant changes in professional attitudes, practices and cultures. Following Professor Kitwood's untimely death at the end of the 1990s, the mantle of developing person-centred care was taken up by Professor Dawn Brooker who, at the time, was also working out of the Bradford Dementia Group in the UK. In a subsequent influential paper, Brooker (2004) developed the VIPS model of person-centred care:

- Value of all human lives;
- Individualised approach recognising uniqueness;
- seeing the world from the Perspective of the service user;
- Social environment that promotes well-being.

The VIPS model provides a helpful memory aide highlighting the importance and value of people living with dementia as well as reflecting a more holistic appreciation of the relationships that infuse daily life. In a later text, Brooker and Latham (2015) extended the reach of the VIPs model to challenge the prevailing culture of care home attitudes and outlined the importance of 'getting person-centred care into everyday practice' (p. 24). Whilst the importance of the application of the biopsychosocial model to clinical practice has been outlined (Revolta et al., 2016), the statement presumes that that the model was complete. However, following a collective case study design, Keady et al. (2013) added a 'physical' dimension in an adaptation to the biopsychosocial model so that it became presented as the bio-psycho-social-physical model of dementia. The physical domain was seen to comprise of five domains which Keady et al. (2013) identified as: (i) physical well-being; (ii) physical health and examination; (iii) physical care; (iv) physical treatment and (v) physical environment. Amongst other considerations, the expansion of the biopsychosocial model enabled the physical environment to be considered as a contributing factor to developing a broader understanding about the meaning of health to a person living with dementia. This addition might prove useful to researchers and others when developing design opportunities in dementia care and practice.

Citizenship and human rights

Whilst both Kitwood's and Brooker's separate contributions to developing and testing a theory of dementia is significant (see also: Kitwood and Brooker, 2019), commentators have highlighted some deficits. Firstly, the outlined theory of personhood and person-centred care failed to adequately account for the active role that people living with dementia play in shaping their own lives and secondly, personhood is rooted to care settings rather than in the everyday spaces of the domestic home and/or neighbourhood. To counter this imbalance, Bartlett and O'Connor (2010) put forward ideas around social citizenship to describe the ways in which people living with dementia can remain active citizens and underpinned social citizenship with an ongoing rights-based approach, as seen in their definition:

> Social citizenship can be defined as a relationship, practice or status, in which a person with dementia is entitled to experience freedom from discrimination, and to have opportunities to grow and participate in life to the fullest extent possible. It involves justice, recognition of social positions, rights and a fluid degree of responsibility for shaping events at a personal and societal level.
>
> (p. 37)

Developing a theory of dementia through a rights-based approach has been picked up and developed by people living with dementia themselves (Mental Health Foundation, 2015) and adopted by the World Health Organisation (WHO) in their global action plan on the public health response to dementia (WHO, 2017). As an illustration, in England, the Dementia Action Alliance has outlined five 'Dementia Statements' that people living with dementia believe are essential to upholding their everyday quality of life:

- We have the right to be recognised as who we are, to make choices about our lives including taking risks, and to contribute to society. Our diagnosis should not define us, nor should we be ashamed of it.
- We have the right to continue with day to day and family life, without discrimination or unfair cost, to be accepted and included in our communities and not live in isolation or loneliness.
- We have the right to an early and accurate diagnosis, and to receive evidence-based, appropriate, compassionate and properly funded care and treatment, from trained people who understand us and how dementia affects us. This must meet our needs, wherever we live.
- We have the right to be respected, and recognised as partners in care, provided with education, support, services, and training which enables us to plan and make decisions about the future.
- We have the right to know about and decide if we want to be involved in research that looks at cause, cure and care for dementia and be supported to take part.

(for further information see: www.dementiaaction.org.uk/news/23236_news_launching_the_dementia_statements; accessed 7 June 2020).

As current policy and practice strategies develop to take account of the everyday lives of people with dementia, a rights-based approach to social

Table 2.1 13-item core outcome set – what matters most to people with dementia living at home

1. Continuing good relationships with people who are important to you
2. Being able to communicate with others
3. Feeling safe and secure at home
4. Feeling valued and respected by others
5. Being able to do things that you enjoy and want to keep doing
6. Keeping interested in things you like
7. Being aware of your surroundings indoors and outdoors
8. Being able to find your way around a familiar place
9. Being as clean and comfortable as you would like
10. Not falling at home or when out and about
11. Being able to see, hear and understand
12. Feeling able to keep your identity
13. Feeling able to have a laugh with other people

Source: Reilly et al. (2020).

citizenship that embodies such relational qualities may well be a foundation on which to build lasting change (Cahill, 2018). To augment this direction, Reilly et al. (2020) have recently published a 13-item core outcome set that addressed what matters most to people with dementia living at home. The 13-item core outcome set (written from the perspective of people living with dementia) is shown in Table 2.1.

The research design underpinning the development of the 13-item core outcome set involved people living with dementia at all points, including in the adapted Delphi technique (Reilly et al., 2020). Whilst useful in their own right, arguably the statements in Table 2.1 could be used to formulate and evaluate community-based care for people living with dementia and in framing practice and design opportunities. From work to date, the most relevant instrument to measure the 13 statements in Table 2.1 is the 'Engagement and Independence in Dementia Questionnaire (EID-Q)' (Stoner et al., 2018; and see Harding et al., 2020) where 7 of the 13 statements are covered. However, room for improvement exists and is a future challenge to the design and the dementia studies field.

Interestingly, each of the 13 statements in Table 2.1 also closely map onto the concept of social health in dementia. To develop this point further, social health is a concept that people living with dementia have endorsed as relevant and meaningful to their everyday lives and is directed towards three main areas: firstly, the capacity to fulfil one's potential and obligations; secondly, the ability to manage life with some degree of independence; and thirdly, participation in social activities (Dröes et al., 2017). Pointing towards a new direction for dementia care research and practice, social health and everyday citizenship can be expressed through dementia-friendly community practices and social relationships (Nedlund et al., 2019), issues that are highly pertinent to this book and its direction.

Conclusion

This chapter has provided a broad overview of the dementia field and has provided a context to enable the developments in design and dementia to be located. The importance of people living with dementia seeking agency and retaining control of their lived experience is a direction that will be built upon in the remaining chapters as it overspills into the methodological areas of co-production and co-design, for example. We would see meeting these new directions as crucial pointers to representing lived experience whilst holding true to the value that people living with dementia are individuals each with a unique life story and biography.

References

Allison, R. S. (1962). *The Senile Brain: A Clinical Study*. London: Edward Arnold.

All-Party Parliamentary Group on Dementia (2016). *Dementia rarely travels alone. Living with dementia and other conditions*. Available: www.alzheimers.org.uk/sites/default/files/migrate/downloads/appg_on_dementia_2 016_report.pdf; accessed 7 June 2020.

Alzheimer, A. (1897). *Beiträge zur pathologischen Anatomie der Hirnrinde und zur anatomischen Grundlage einiger Psychosen. Monatsschr Psychiatry Neurology*, 2: 82–120.

Alzheimer, A. (1907). *Über eine eigenartige Erkankung der Hirnrinde. Allgemeine Zeits Psychiatry, Psychisch-Gerichtlich Medicine*, 64: 146–148.

Alzheimer's Disease International. (2011). *World Alzheimer Report 2011: The Benefits of Early Diagnosis and Intervention*. London: Alzheimer's Disease International.

Alzheimer's Disease International. (2015). *World Alzheimer Report 2015. The Global Impact of Dementia: An Analysis of Prevalence, Incidence, Cost & Trends*. London: Alzheimer Disease International.

Alzheimer's Society. (2014). *Dementia 2014: Opportunity for Change*. London: Alzheimer's Society.

Alzheimer's Society. (2015). *The Progression of Alzheimer's Disease and Other Dementias*. Factsheet 458LP. Available at: www.alzheimers.org.uk/sites/default/files/migrate/downloads/factsheet_the_progression_of_alzheimers_disease_and_other_dementias.pdf; accessed 7 June 2020.

Alzheimer's Society. (2019a). *Dementia UK: 2014 Edition*. London: Alzheimer's Society.

Alzheimer's Society. (2019b). *Facts for the Media*. London: Alzheimer's Society.

American Psychiatric Association. (2013). *Diagnostic and Statistical Manual of Mental Disorders, Fifth Edition (DSM-5)*. Available at: https://dsm.psychiatryonline.org/doi/book/10.1176/appi.books.9780890425596; accessed 7 June 2020.

Bartlett, R. and O'Connor, D. (2010). *Broadening the Dementia Debate: Towards Social Citizenship*. Bristol: Policy Press.

Berrios, G. E. (1987). Dementia during the seventeenth and eighteenth centuries: a conceptual history. *Psychological Medicine*, 17: 829–837.

Berrios, G. E. (1990). Alzheimer's disease: a conceptual history. *International Journal of Geriatric Psychiatry*, 5: 355–365.

Borrell-Carrió, F., Suchman, A. L. and Epstein, R. M. (2004). The biopsychosocial model 25 years later: principles, practice, and scientific inquiry. *Annals of Family Medicine*, 2: 576–582.

Brayne, C. and Calloway, P. (1990). The case identification of dementia in the community: a comparison of methods. *International Journal of Geriatric Psychiatry*, 5: 309–316.

Brooker, D. (2004). What is person centred care in dementia? *Reviews in Clinical Gerontology*, 13: 215–222.

Brooker, D. and Latham, I. (2015). *Person-Centred Dementia Care, Making Services Better with the VIPS Framework*. Second Edition. London: Jessica Kingsley.

Cahill, S. (2018). *Dementia and Human Rights*. Bristol: Policy Press.

Department of Health. (2015). *Prime Minister's Challenge on Dementia 2020*. London: Department of Health.

Department of Health and Social Care. (2020). *COVID-19: Our Action Plan for Adult Social Care*. London: Department of Health.

Dröes, R. M., Chattat, R., Diaz, A., Gove, D., Graff, M., Murphy, K., Verbeek, H., Vernooij-Dassen, M., Clare, L., Johannessen, A., Roes, M., Verhey, F. and Charras, K. (2017). Social health and dementia: a European consensus on the operationalization of the concept and directions for research and practice. *Aging & Mental Health*, 21 (1): 4–17.

Engel, G. L. (1977). The need for a new medical model: a challenge for biomedicine. *Science*, 196: 129–136.

Engel, G. L. (1980). The clinical application of the biopsychosocial model. *American Journal of Psychiatry*, 137: 535–544.

Erol, R., Brooker, D. and Peel, E. (2016). The impact of dementia on women internationally: an integrative review. *Health Care for Women International*, 37 (12): 1320–1341.

Gerritsen, A. A. J., Bakker, C., Verhey, F. R. J., Pijnenburg, Y. A. L., Millenaar, J. K., de Vugt, M. E. and Koopmans, R. T. C. M. (2019). Survival and life-expectancy in a young-onset dementia cohort with six years of follow-up: the NeedYD-study. *International Psychogeriatrics*, 31(12): 1781–1789.

Ghaemi, S. N. (2010). *The Rise and Fall of the Biopsychosocial Model: Reconciling Art and Science in Psychiatry*. JHU Press, New York, NY.

Goldberg, T. E., Kleinman, J. E., Daniel, D.G., Myslobodsky, M. S., Ragland, J. D. and Weinberger, D. R. (1988). Dementia praecox revisited: age disorientation, mental status, and ventricular enlargement. *British Journal of Psychiatry*, 153: 187–190.

Harding, A., Morbey, H., Ahmed, F., Opdebeeck, C., Elvish, R., Leroi, I., Williamson, P., Keady, J. and Reilly, S. (2020). Core outcome set for non-pharmacological community-based interventions for people living with dementia at home: A systematic review of outcome measurement instruments. *The Gerontologist*, Published on-line first and available at: gnaa071, doi.org: 10.1093/geront/gnaa071.

James, I. A. and Jackman, L. (2017). *Understanding Behaviour in Dementia that Challenges. A Guide to Assessment and Treatment*. Second Edition. London: Jessica Kingsley Publishers.

Keady, J. and Jones, L. (2010). Investigating the causes of behaviours that challenge in people with dementia. *Nursing Older People*, 22 (9): 25–29.

Keady, J., Jones, L., Ward, R., Koch, S., Swarbrick, C., Hellström, I., Davies-Quarrell, V. and Williams, S. (2013). Introducing the bio-psycho-social-physical model of dementia through a collective case study design. *Journal of Clinical Nursing*, 22 (19–20): 2768–2777.

Kitwood, T. (1988). The technical, the personal and the framing of dementia. *Social Behaviour*, 3: 161–180.

Kitwood, T. (1990a). Understanding senile dementia: a psychobiographical approach. *Free Associations*, 1: 60–76.

Kitwood, T. (1990b). The dialectics of dementia: with particular reference to Alzheimer's disease. *Ageing and Society*, 10 (2): 177–196.

Kitwood, T. (1997). *Dementia Reconsidered: The Person Comes First*. Buckingham: Open University.

Kitwood, T. and Bredin, M. (1992a). Towards a theory of dementia care: personhood and well-being. *Ageing and Society*, 12: 269–287.

Kitwood, T. and Bredin, K. (1992b). A new approach to the evaluation of dementia care. *Journal of Advances in Health and Nursing Care*, 1 (5): 41–60.

Kitwood, T. (original author, 1997) and Brooker, D. (Ed.). (2019). *Dementia Reconsidered-Revisited: The Person Still Comes First*. Buckingham: Open University.

Loza, N. and Milad, G. (1990). Notes from ancient Egypt. *International Journal of Geriatric Psychiatry*, 5: 403–405.

Marcé, L. V. (1863). Recherches cliniques et anatomo-pathologiques sur la démence senile et sur les differences qui la separent de la paralysis générale. *Gazette Medicale de Paris*, 34: 433–435

Marinesco, G. (1900). Mécanisme da la sénilitié et de la mort des cellules nerveuses. CR Hebdomad. *Seances Academic Scientifique*, 130: 1136–1139.

Mental Health Foundation. (2015). *Dementia, Rights and the Social Model of Disability*. London: Mental Health Foundation.

Moniz-Cook, E., Hart, C., Woods, B., Whitaker, C., James, I., Russell, I., Tudor, E. R., Hilton, A., Orrell, M., Campion, P., Stokes, G., Jones, R. S. P., Bird, M., Poland, F. and Manthorpe, J. (2017). Challenge Demcare: management of challenging behaviour in dementia at home and in care homes – development, evaluation and implementation of an online individualised intervention for care homes; and a cohort study of specialist community mental health care for families. *NIHR Programme Grants for Applied Research*, 5(15): doi: 10.3310/pgfar05150; accessed 7 June 2020.

Neugebauer, R. (1978). Treatment of the mentally ill in medieval and early modern England: a reappraisal. *Journal of History and Behavioural Science*, 14: 158–169.

National Institute for Health and Care Excellence. (2018). *Dementia: Assessment, Management and Support for People Living with Dementia and Their Carers*. NICE guideline. Available: www.nice.org.uk/guidance/ng97; accessed 7 June 2020.

National Institute for Health and Clinical Excellence/Social Care Institute for Excellence. (2006). *Dementia: Supporting People with Dementia and Their Carers in Health and Social Care. NICE Clinical Practice Guideline 42.* London: National Institute for Health and Clinical Excellence.

Nedlund, A. C., Bartlett, R. and Clarke, C. L. (2019). *Everyday Citizenship and People with Dementia*. Edinburgh: Dunedin.

O'Sullivan, D., O'Regan, N. A. and Timmons, S. (2016). Validity and reliability of the 6-item cognitive impairment test for screening cognitive impairment: a review. *Dementia and Geriatric Cognitive Disorders*, 42: 42–49.

Pinel, P. (1787). *Nosographie Philosophique*. Fifth Edition. Paris: Brosson.

Reilly, S. T., Harding, A. J. E., Morbey, H., Ahmed, F., Williamson, P. R., Swarbrick, C., Leroi, I., Davies, L., Reeves, D., Holland, F., Hann, M. and Keady, J. (2020). What is important to people with dementia living at home? A set of core outcome items for use in the evaluation of non-pharmacological community-based health and social care interventions. *Age and Ageing*, 1–8. doi: 10.1093/ageing/afaa.

Reisberg, B., Ferris, S. H., deLeon, M. J. and Crook, T. (1988). Global deterioration scale (GDS). *Psychopharmacology Bulletin*, 24 (4): 661–664

Revolta, C., Orrell, M. and Spector, A. (2016). The biopsychosocial (BPS) model of dementia as a tool for clinical practice. A pilot study. *International Psychogeriatrics*, 28 (7): 1079–1089.

Sabat, S. R. (2008). "A bio-psycho-social approach to dementia." In Downs, M. and Bowers, B. (Eds.) *Excellence in Dementia Care: Research into Practice*, pp. 70–84. Maidenhead: Open University Press.

Sabat, S. R. (2011). A Bio-Psycho-Social model enhances young adults' understanding of and beliefs about people with Alzheimer's disease: a case study. *Dementia: The International Journal of Social Research and Practice*, 11 (1): 95–112.

Sabat, S. R. and Harré, R. (1994). The Alzheimer's disease sufferer as a semiotic subject. *Philosophy, Psychiatry, and Psychology*, 1: 145–160.

Sabat, S. R., Johnson, A., Swarbrick C. and Keady, J. (2011). The 'demented other' or simply 'a person'? Extending the philosophical discourse of Ursula Naue and Thilo Kroll through an appreciation of the situated self. *Nursing Philosophy*, 12: 282–292.

Samsi, K., Abley, C., Campbell, S., Keady, J., Manthorpe, J., Robinson, L., Watts, S. and Bond, J. (2014). Negotiating a Labyrinth: experiences of assessment and diagnostic journey in cognitive impairment and dementia. *International Journal of Geriatric Psychiatry*, 29(1): 58–67.

Skultans, V. (1979). *English Madness*. London: Routledge and Kegan Paul.

Stoner, C. R., Orrell, M., and Spector, A. (2018). Psychometric properties and factor analysis of the Engagement and independence in dementia questionnaire (EID-Q). *Dementia and Geriatric Cognitive Disorders*, 46 (3–4): 119–127.

Wolters, F. J., Tinga, L. M., Dhana, K., Koudstaal, P. J., Hofman, A., Bos, D., Franco, O. H. and Ikram, M. A. (2019). Life expectancy with and without dementia: a population-based study of dementia burden and preventive potential. *American Journal of Epidemiology*, 188 (2): 372–381.

World Health Organisation. (2017). *Global Action Plan on the Public Health Response to Dementia*. Geneva: World Health Organisation.

3 Contexts

Design challenges

Diagnosis

As seen in Chapter 2, reaching a diagnosis of dementia is the first step in formally recognizing that a person is living with the condition and should therefore receive appropriate care to slow down the progression of the disease (if at all possible) and improve their quality of life. However, dementia is currently under-detected, under-diagnosed, under-disclosed, under-treated and under-managed in primary care (Prince et al., 2016).

Part of the challenge lies on how the term for 'dementia' has been defined. A standard criterion for dementia is that cognitive impairment is sufficiently severe to compromise social and occupational functioning and that memory must be specifically impaired (Rossor et al., 2010). This often results in a delay in a specific diagnosis of the cause of the dementia. Thus, before a person living with dementia can be diagnosed using these criteria, the disease will be well advanced (Rossor et al., 2010).

Age poses an additional challenge in reaching a diagnosis of dementia. This is because the oldest-old are the fastest growing segment of the population and have the highest rates of dementia. However, the diagnosis of dementia in this age group is further complicated by naturally occurring age-related phenomena such as sensory losses, medical co-morbidities, over-medication use and frailty (Brumback-Peltz et al., 2011). On the other hand, diagnosis of dementia in younger age groups – also known as 'early onset dementia' – is equally challenging as its symptoms are not easily associated with the condition (Rossor et al., 2010). The challenges faced by individuals living with early onset dementia and by those who support and care for them are different due to the stage of life that is interrupted by the diagnosis and the duration of the disease course (Lambert et al., 2014). For this group of younger people living with dementia, employability, current family dynamics and presentation of dementia symptoms can intensify experiences and increase stress for them and their families (Roach et al., 2016). Indeed, it can take over one and a half years longer to be diagnosed for people living with early onset dementia as compared to people over the age of 65 (Greenwood and Smith, 2016). This questions whether the same clinical and neuropathological criteria used for the diagnosis of dementia on older populations can be applied for on the oldest-old populations as well as in younger populations (Slavin et al., 2013). Diagnosis is seen as a significant point of transition in the dementia journey (Slavin et al., 2013; Lambert et al., 2014; Roach et al., 2016). There is also a recognised lack of information coupled with frustration during this transition period especially when some providers are reluctant to investigate dementia as a first line of inquiry, especially if the person/patient is of younger age (Roach et al., 2016). The overwhelming sense of uncertainty around getting a diagnosis, and the fact that initial contacts with doctors and healthcare providers are often a struggle, are reasons why a diagnosis may be delayed or not even attempted in the first place (Samsi et al., 2014).

Better communication can assist in building trust and shed light on the problems experienced to allow them to be addressed appropriately (Alsaeed et al., 2016). This includes more guided information and education on available strategies and devices and a continuous assessment of needs for both the carer and the person living with dementia to support them throughout the journey (Soilemezi et al., 2017). This is an area where design researchers, especially those with expertise in communication design, can make a difference. Furthermore, researchers with expertise in interior, architecture and spatial design can make a significant contribution, as there is a need to reach both people living with dementia and their caregivers in time and increase their awareness of potential environmental strategies, and how to manipulate the environment in different ways and at different stages of the condition (Soilemezi et al., 2017).

Care

Dementia gradually challenges a person's capacity to communicate with others. However, this diminishing capacity to communicate is not only because of the person living with dementia's limited cognitive and semantic deficits (i.e. failing episodic memory). The key communicative challenges people living with dementia face are due to lack of interaction with others (Jones, 2015). Thus, any interventions or activities that encourage social interaction with others, is critical and an area that can be explored by design research further.

In addition to this, from what is known about procedural memory, we might expect that even when people living with dementia do not know that they have done an activity (such as being unable to remember or explain their involvement), they may still know how to do it (Phinney et al., 2007). People living with dementia need more support than so-called 'healthy' older people do and they are less likely to use conscious strategies even when supervised (Nygård, 2004). This is a capacity issue that could be supported by the design of a familiar environment, based on familiar activities and drawing on biographical memories or remembered life storylines. Design research could clearly contribute in the environment design, but it can also identify strategies that people living with dementia initiate and use without conscious implementation in their daily activities. In achieving this, it is equally important to involve caregivers and family members in both the research and the design of the strategies, in order to provide better care support.

Multiple co-morbidities and the care environment

It is well recognised that several people living with dementia may have multiple co-morbidities – a secondary or additional disease or disorder that a person may have, such as mental and chronic physical health conditions such as hypertension and diabetes (Thuné-Boyle et al., 2010; George et al., 2013; APPG, 2016; Prince et al., 2016). To make matters worse, a number of co-morbidities are often undiagnosed (Poblador-Plou et al., 2014) and complications associated with these are common (Thuné-Boyle et al., 2010). These bring challenges for healthcare professional, caregivers and researchers.

People living with dementia are more likely to be admitted to general hospital than people of similar age and medical infirmity. Several of these conditions are preventable such as falls, fractured hips, urinary infections and chest infections (Prince et al., 2016; Scrutton and Brancati, 2016). Given the high chances of prolonged hospitalization of people living with dementia, the design of the hospital environment and services to best cater for them becomes essential. For individuals living with dementia, sensitivity to lighting and noise levels may be exacerbated by the hearing and visual deficits associated with ageing, thereby making it difficult for them to understand their surrounding environment (Prince et al., 2016). This is a particular challenge, as frequently the medical aspects of dementia are over-emphasised in hospital in comparison with the emotional and psychological aspects (George et al., 2013).

The role of the environment in the care of people living with dementia extends beyond formal care settings, such as hospitals. More precisely, as people living with dementia have heightened sensitivity to environmental stressors and cues, it is vital that the designed environment is appropriate and responsive to their cognitive abilities and functioning (Chaudhury and Cooke, 2014; Førsund et al., 2018). There is a growing literature on the practical aspects of design of the care environment to enhance the safety of people living with dementia and the role of the environment in care (George et al., 2013; Nehen and Hermann, 2015).

The presence of co-morbidities also makes people living with dementia particularly vulnerable to adverse outcomes of hospitalization. Furthermore, as often the person living with dementia, especially at the more advanced stages, cannot communicate verbally, or solve problems, or provide valid consent to procedures, care decisions might involve proxy decision-makers such as family members (Chang et al., 2009). This necessitates ensuring that people living with dementia admitted for any clinical reason receive high quality and safe care (George et al., 2013).

Considering the multifaceted physical, cognitive and psychosocial challenges people living with dementia face, there is a need for a holistic and comprehensive way to address cognitive and functional disabilities, to prevent and treat newly emerging behavioural symptoms, and to optimise quality of life (Nehen and Hermann, 2015). In doing so it is imperative to take into account for the preferences of people living with dementia and their caregivers, in order to reduce burden on people living with dementia, and improve their quality of life (Prince et al., 2016).

Medicine management and administration

Challenges to medicines use are centred on medicine administration, management and their impact on the caregiver and care recipient, their partnership and interface with formal care (Alsaeed et al., 2016). The poor memory which impacts people living with dementia, means that family caregivers have to often take on the responsibility of administering medicines, managing side effects, and maintaining the medicinal supply. This can sometimes generate stress and negatively impacts the caregiver's quality of life, especially if the caregiver is a partner of the person living with dementia and of a certain age, and are also more likely to take medicines regularly. In such circumstances, caregivers may need to arrange their own medication schedule to correspond with that of the person they are caring for.

Additional challenges often also include adhering to complicated instructions, such as how to give medicines, and making decisions on when to withhold or give medicines. This is further exacerbated when the person living with dementia is experiencing several health conditions (co-morbidities) and has thus to manage several medications on a daily basis (Alsaeed et al., 2016). Evidently, the provision of clear information regarding medicines is vital and an area where communication product and packaging designers can focus further research, as future research should focus on developing targeted interventions that can overcome these challenges to achieve optimal medicine use (Alsaeed et al., 2016).

Caregiver challenges and well-being

The extent to which the process of providing care to a family member living with dementia affects the physical and mental health of the caregiver has received a great deal of attention in the literature (Connell et al., 2001; Silva et al., 2013; Nehen and Hermann, 2015). Generally, it is widely recognized that caring for an older, disabled relative, particularly one with cognitive or mental health problems, can have adverse effects on the caregiver's own physical and mental health (Zarit and Femia, 2008; Xiao et al., 2014). In the case of dementia, the evidence linking caregiving to negative mental health outcomes is compelling and consistent (Connell et al., 2001). Caring for people living with dementia has long been associated with increased levels of depression, anxiety (Connell et al., 2001; Nehen and Hermann, 2015) and reduced quality of life (Silva et al., 2013).

Looking at caring for people living with dementia more closely, it is mostly spouses or children who are taking on the caregiver role, although the impact of the diagnosis wanes on family members and children who may still be in early childhood (Lambert et al., 2014). The challenges family members face in managing their relative's condition are multifaceted. Particularly, the high load of supervision and care causes psychosocial distress both for the caregivers and people living with dementia that affects the partner's health state (Nehen and Hermann, 2015). As caring for people living with dementia requires considerable amount of time, the caregiver's social and professional lives may also be disrupted. Caregivers spend less time socializing and interacting with other, further increasing their distress and mental health (Thuné-Boyle et al., 2010). Moreover, as their family member's autonomy and cognition decline, caregivers often face increasing challenges. These relate to management of the person living with dementia's medication, as discussed earlier, and also the management of the family member's diet. Their employment is also disrupted (Silva et al., 2013), thus impacting on household resources and on support both for themselves and for family members (Lambert et al., 2014). The challenges and level of emotional burden the primary caregiver experiences can be lowered the more family members share care, as findings of a study by Xiao et al. (2014) show.

Although in most Western societies it is the adult children and spouses of people living with dementia who are assuming the caregiving role, the norms for care provision are greatly influenced by culture and ethnicity (Connell et al., 2001). Culture has an influence on gender and a family member's role in care of older people. Studies have identified that a caregiver of a spouse who was female experienced significantly higher subjective burden than a male who was a non-spouse (Xiao et al., 2014).

Studies such as that of Xiao et al. (2014) that have compared dementia family caregiver perceptions across different countries have found that culture plays an active role in the subjective burden experienced by caregivers. When comparing Chinese and Australian caregivers, they found that acceptance of cultural norms influenced by collectivism and filial piety decreased caregiver's subjective burden. Whilst a higher subjective burden was observed in Australia, where the influence of individualistic culture (i.e. independence, socialization) was present (Xiao et al., 2014; Koo et al., 2020). This suggests that collectivistic cultures may be a counter factor of subjective burdens.

The issue of dementia caregiving has important policy implications, as the negative health outcomes can compromise the ability of family members to provide continued care and reduce their employment. There is therefore a need requiring further research attention.

Social transformation and dementia care

The rapid social transformations we are experiencing across the world today are also affecting dementia care. The social transformation is weakening the family care model, affecting dementia care especially in countries with undeveloped dementia services (Wang et al., 2014). The phenomenon of job mobility which has become the norm in the developed world, is now evident in developing countries, such as Malaysia, India, China and several others.

The internal migration triggered by the opportunities for better employment in urban settings and the improved social status of women in the workforce, who were traditionally home-based in previous generations, are challenging the traditional family role of caring for people living with dementia (Xiao et al., 2014). In countries such as China, the 'one-child policy' and the decreasing family size in developed countries, such as Japan, result in the family assuming less responsibility towards care of elderly people, including the growing number of older adults living with dementia (Chen et al., 2014).

In developed countries, such as Australia, caring for older people is seen as part of social welfare with dementia services for older people being funded and regulated by the government. In contrast, in developing countries like China, caring for older people is viewed as a family's responsibility, hence as there is such importance on families providing care of older people, dementia care services are consequently undeveloped as compared to Western societies (Xiao et al., 2014).

At present, there is currently a shift in developed countries, such as the UK, Netherlands, etc. in reducing rates of hospitalisation for people living with dementia, due to the high costs of hospital admission (Prince et al., 2016). This will result in increasing community-based and outreach services that are resource-intensive. However, currently the care associated costs are yet to be shifted from acute hospital to community health and social care, placing extra financial burden on family caregivers (Wang et al., 2014; Prince et al., 2016).

Therefore, it is evident that as developed nations are shifting dementia care from formal to informal structures, from healthcare to community health settings, societal transformations in developing nations are leading to take steps towards the opposite. This creates a need for care service redesign and new policy development; as a consequence, there are opportunities for service designers and design policy researchers to be involved in this care transformation.

Quality of life

Improving the quality of life of people living with dementia and their caregivers forms a key research priority and area of focus. Therefore, several important contextual themes are explored and discussed in this section and under the following headings.

Young-onset dementia and impact on quality of living

The management of young-onset dementia presents challenges that differ from those of older people, especially as they have a more aggressive progression of the disease in comparison (Rossor et al., 2010). More precisely, people living with young-onset dementia face unique social challenges, which go beyond those of older people living with dementia, resulting in an even greater negative impact on their lives (Greenwood and Smith, 2016). Beyond the financial impact people living with young-onset dementia experience, it is the loss of meaningful activity, disempowerment and reduced social contact after job loss that impacts them the most (Greenwood and Smith, 2016).

There are several implications also to families of people living with young-onset dementia who have even more difficulties than the family members of the elderly living with dementia (Johannessen and Möller, 2013). Maintaining autonomy and a sense of purpose is very important to people living with young-onset dementia (Greenwood and Smith, 2016), as it benefits not only the individual person but also their family (Roach et al., 2016).

In supporting this, those caring for people living with young-onset dementia should avoid being over-protective, even if the abilities of the person living with dementia are reduced or lost. Taking part in meaningful activity and inclusion in society is important. Therefore, it is imperative to provide them with services of different kinds at an early stage, especially ones that support keeping in touch with society (Johannessen and Möller, 2013). These could be provided by the voluntary sector (Greenwood and Smith, 2016) but also in the workplace. Currently individualised, suitable work tasks adapted for people living with young-onset dementia are rarely arranged resulting in early exit from the workforce (Johannessen and Möller, 2013).

Social isolation

Improving the quality of life for people living with dementia is widely accepted as an important outcome in dementia care services. As dementia care turns towards the enhancement of quality of life, both research and practice developments require to account for the variables that contribute to the well-being in dementia (Wolverson et al., 2010).

Social isolation and transitions out of the home form key challenges for people living with dementia (Roach et al., 2016). More precisely, it has been demonstrated that the ability to initiate and maintain interactions with other people declines as dementia progresses (Ekström et al., 2017). People living with dementia face difficulties in both initiating and maintaining social interactions and experience diminished social relationships. As the ability to communicate and interact is crucial for creating and maintaining social relations, a dementia diagnosis increases the risk of being socially excluded. Research has shown clearly that interpersonal and community engagement is important for health maintenance and quality of life (Chen et al., 2014), often contributing to a decreased quality of life for both persons living with dementia and their caregivers (Ekström et al., 2017).

Being active and autonomous

The World Health Organization's 'age-friendly' policy movement and dementia awareness campaign highlight the importance of empowering persons living with dementia to remain autonomous and active citizens of society (Førsund et al., 2018). This is also reflected in evidence from research focusing on people living with dementia. It has been found that the single most important driving force for people living with dementia is being active, doing as much as they possibly can. This includes undertaking a wide range of activities such as leisure pastimes, household chores and social involvements. These activities were meaningful in three ways: through their involvement, participants experienced feelings of pleasure and enjoyment; felt a sense of connection and belonging; and retained a sense of autonomy and personal identity (Phinney et al., 2007). Research shows that it is important to encourage mobility in people living with dementia, even though this may increase the risk of falls (George et al., 2013). Meaningful activity extends also for the family of the person living with dementia as it is an important factor in adjusting to life with dementia and maintaining a quality of life (Roach et al., 2016).

It is, consequently, important to provide opportunities for people with dementia to contribute in meaningful ways (Phinney and Moody, 2011). Achieving this, though, requires certain strategies and environments to be available. For instance, research suggests that people living with dementia adopt strategies that are often intuitive rather than concisely planned (Nygård, 2004). Furthermore, it has been suggested that familiarity of the social and physical environment helps promote involvement in activities, as it provides a sense of continuity for people living with dementia, with implications for their quality of life and personhood (Phinney et al., 2007).

These findings suggest the need for greater understanding concerning how awareness of disability may be experienced and exhibited in the course of daily life occupations in persons living with dementia (Nygård, 2004), in order to develop effective community-based programs that will provide direct support to people living with dementia, especially those in the early stages of their illness (Phinney and Moody, 2011). In realising this, it is important to also introduce policies that encourage health practitioners to develop psychosocial interventions that enable people living with dementia to maintain a full and meaningful life (Wolverson et al., 2010).

Technology: managing of everyday and assistive technology

As technology has entered all aspects of our lives, including healthcare, researchers have begun exploring its use, especially of non-pharmacological interventions in the care of people living with dementia too. The literature and review studies such as that of Lynn et al. (2019) have identified several areas where the use of technology is starting to show positive outcomes, such as in complementing staff care, providing tenants and residents with a sense of security, enabling social interaction, enhancing well-being and promoting independence.

This topic is explored in more detail in Chapter 5, nevertheless we offer here a few examples of how it is utilised in different contexts and some of the challenges also associated with its use. There has been a focus on the use of technology as communication and memory support aid. This is often realized via employing tablet computers to show personal photo albums and videos as tools to enhance the expressive abilities of people living with dementia and encourage communication with caregivers; which in turn has reduced behaviour problems and made participation in everyday activities more meaningful (Ekström et al., 2017). Technology is also utilised by people living with dementia, especially in the early stages of the disease, in order to compensate for cognitive and other deficits and assist with everyday life. This suggests that people with cognitive deficits may be assisted by new technology, or new ways of using familiar technology, to cope with daily life or to compensate for any deficits (Nygård, 2008). However, this requires that they are highly motivated to use the technology and critically that the individuality of each adult living with dementia is considered when designing, developing or supporting technology use. This provides several research opportunities for the design research community.

Technology is, however, not a panacea with studies confirming that older adults living with dementia experience difficulties in managing everyday technology (Nygård, 2008) as well as the presence of several challenges associated with the use of technology-based interventions for people living with dementia. These include interventions such as false alarms, reliability, alarm fatigue, staff fear and reluctance to use technology (Niemeijer et al., 2015), cost and their acceptance by the person living with dementia (Lynn et al., 2019).

The physical environment and home adaptation

The physical environment is a critical component of a therapeutic setting for people living with dementia. Persons living with dementia experience a reduction in their lived space as dementia develops. Førsund et al. (2018) use the metaphor of the Russian babushka doll to describe the experiences of persons with dementia living in a space where lived space gradually becomes smaller. Researching the home environment and ageing-in-place has increasingly become the focus of dementia care and is crucial for a number of reasons, including reducing care costs, providing a familiar and meaningful space for people (Soilemezi et al., 2017).

Belonging, meaningfulness, security and autonomy are essential elements of the experience of lived space among persons living with dementia (Førsund et al., 2018) and the literature has shown that a well-designed supportive physical environment can foster positive behaviours, such as reduced agitation, increased social contact and less dependence in conducting activities of daily living (Chaudhury and Cooke, 2014). In contrast, unsupportive physical environments can contribute to common challenging behaviours, especially as facing new environments threatens a person's ability to uphold a sense of control over one's own life, safety and meaning. Thus, enabling people living with dementia to stay in their home environments, can help prevent physical illnesses, hospitalization and further deterioration (Nehen and Hermann, 2015).

Living with dementia at home and supporting this for as long as possible form important objectives for researchers and policy-makers. This requires adaptation or re-design of the home environment in order to increase accessibility. Although some of these home environmental interventions may require some financial investment, there are also several easily implemented and low-cost strategies (e.g. labelling cupboards, covering mirrors) that can be applied (Soilemezi et al., 2017). This can, for example, include facilitating the perceptual input from the environment and providing the opportunity to practise existing habits and routines without making intrusive environmental adaptations and by explicitly taking the person's own preferences and use of cues and arrangements in the environment adaptation design (Nygård, 2004). Hence the opportunities for designers and architects in this context are immense as is the role they can play in the design of a safe, accessible, friendly and supportive home environment design for people living with dementia and their family caregivers.

Research and ethics

Involving people living with dementia in research raises many ethical and practical issues for people living with dementia, carers and family members, researchers and care professionals (Sherratt et al., 2007; McKeown et al., 2010; Gray et al., 2017). A paradox is observed here, as although there are millions of people living with dementia worldwide, only a fraction of these individuals take part in research (Gray et al., 2017; Bartlett et al., 2018). This extends to not only including people living with dementia in the development, implementation and evaluation of activities but also in involving consulting them in relevant research activities.

This is a challenge not only for research into treatments and interventions for people living with dementia and studies of the incidence and prevalence of dementia, but also for observational and qualitative studies (Bartlett et al., 2018). This raises concerns about the effectiveness of research which does not include those with the condition in the trialling or piloting of them. In the face of this challenge and absence of dementia voice from the literature, there is, in recent years, a growing body of research that describes the subjective experiences of people living with dementia in the context of their everyday lives (Phinney and Moody, 2011). This is an area that although currently dominated predominantly by social science, it can be enhanced and diversified by design research, especially through the use of creative and visual methods that can help record and depict better the lived experiences. We will return to this issue in the next chapter.

Caregiver involvement in research

There are several barriers which may prevent people living with dementia from participating in studies. These range from lack of awareness about research opportunities to the commitment of a study partner, typically a family caregiver in the research (Bartlett et al., 2018). More precisely, conducting research that involves people living with dementia especially in the mild/middle stages requires also the frequent involvement of their spouse or child or other family caregiver. This is challenging particularly for younger caregivers, such as adult children who are more likely to be working and have additional obligations. With respect to this, evidence shows those living with dementia are less likely to participate in research if they have a non-spouse caregiver and the few who do are more likely to drop out (Brodaty and Donkin, 2009; Grill et al., 2013). This suggests that different recruitment approaches are needed and that consideration of relationship status may be important when seeking to recruit a person living with dementia to any study (Bartlett et al., 2018).

The latter highlights the importance of family caregivers as gatekeepers to recruitment of people living with dementia in research. This clearly requires considerable work and planning and in negotiating research access to people living with dementia. Considering the wider range of gatekeepers beyond the immediate family, such as practitioners, managers, ethics committees and other professional carers, the task of participant recruitment becomes even more complex and challenging. This demonstrates that the recruitment process and the design of ethics information material have to be designed for the diverse range of gatekeepers, as recruiting participants may depend on how the gatekeeper perceives the research, the type of relationship they have with potential participants and their personal judgement about who should be involved (McKeown et al., 2010; Bartlett et al., 2018). This in turn raises additional research concerns, regarding the recruitment process and ethics consent.

Informed consent

Informed consent, as practised today, often poses a challenge for involving people living with dementia in research. Today, informed consent is based on a required minimum level of cognitive competence assessed in a way that is generally both clinical and non-situational specific (Dewing, 2007). A diagnosis of dementia does not necessarily indicate incapacity to give consent to be involved in research, as capacity to consent is largely situational and dependent on the complexity of the decision to be made. As dementia progresses, however, it is accepted that abilities of comprehension, making judgements, reasoning, communicating and remembering may become increasingly impaired and thereby capacity to informed consent may be affected (McKeown et al., 2010).

This, consequently, results in persons living with dementia becoming excluded from being involved in research as active participants, as ethics committees may feel it is practically too difficult to involve or the risks are too great (Dewing, 2007; Gray et al., 2017). In light of this the method of proxy consent is being employed. Proxy consent is common in bio-medical research when people living with dementia are deemed legally not able to give informed consent (Moore and Hollett, 2003; McKeown et al., 2010).

It has been claimed that proxy consent still provides a means by which family and professional caregivers, who know well the person living with dementia, can speak on behalf of them and base the decision on their best interests, taking into consideration past desires and values. However, it is found that, on one hand, many persons living with dementia value the opportunity to be heard and to contribute to a research effort and that they wish to continue speaking about their experiences even when strong emotions surface (Moore and Hollett, 2003). And on the other hand, communication with carers of people living with dementia suggests that they are often surprised at the choices their relatives make with regard to diet or participation in activities, compared to the past, so it is difficult to ensure that other values and preferences remain the same with the experience of dementia (McKeown et al., 2010). This demonstrates that there may be a potential conflict between people living with dementia and their proxies when consenting to research and that involving directly people living with dementia is still the most genuine way of them giving voice and contributing to research.

Different ways of including the voice of people living with dementia in research

Hearing the voice of people living with dementia, especially the perspectives and the subjective experiences of older people living with dementia are in recent years been increasingly explored. However, this has proved problematic as the discursive capacity of people living with dementia to articulate meaning maybe impaired (Hubbard et al., 2003).

Communication skills are particularly important here, and training of the specific ways in which individuals can effectively communicate with cognitively impaired people in order to gain accurate information, identify problems and formulate tailored management plans and decisions should be common practice (George et al., 2013). Interviews have been traditionally employed by researchers to ascertain the subjective experience of people living with dementia. Joint interviews with both the person living with dementia and a family member have been also employed as a method that can promote safety and a sense of protection for interviewees living with dementia.

However, they pose the challenge of interfering with individuals' voices being heard (Pesonen et al., 2011). In light of difficulties in verbal communication, considerable attention has been paid to the use of observation in contrast to interviews. Observation enables researchers to better understand and map the perspectives of people living with dementia, especially those whose ability to communicate using conventional means has been affected (Hubbard et al., 2003). Given the diversity of non-verbal and observation-based methods design researchers employ in practice, this challenge area of communication presents opportunities for adopting and adapting design research methods to enable persons' living with dementia voices being heard and subjective experiences being better explored and understood.

Other challenges

Several other challenges exist which do not fall in one of the aforementioned themes and are outlined here. Family can contribute greatly to improving the quality of life for the person living with dementia through their presence, as well as informing staff of what the person living with dementia might desire to improve their quality of living. A challenge here requiring further consideration is the engagement of families in care of people living with dementia (Moyle and Murfield, 2013).

Also, another challenging aspect for caregivers is dealing with the neuro-psychiatric symptoms of dementia, such as agitation, wandering, restlessness and apathy (Soilemezi et al., 2017). Research reviews are examining non-pharmacological interventions to support people living with dementia and their caregivers, however a key challenge of non-pharmacological healthcare studies is the complex nature of therapeutic interventions, which even in the presence of high levels of effectiveness makes it difficult to identify which active elements are responsible for treatment success (Brumback-Peltz et al., 2011).

On another note, as a person's living with dementia communicative abilities decline, it becomes increasingly difficult to ensure that their views are heard impacting, in turn, next of kin and caregiver staff who face ethical dilemmas when it is no longer possible to understand their wishes. Such communication problems affect the possibility for people living with dementia to participate and present their needs and wishes for support in different assessment processes, and thereby, in a sense, to practise their citizenship (Ekström et al., 2017).

Lastly, dementia has a negative impact on the person's nutritional status. People living with dementia often face problems including lack of appetite and altered food preferences which may cause significant weight loss and a subsequent increase in the risk of mortality (Silva et al., 2013).

Summary

This chapter has explored and discussed the challenges people living with dementia face in different aspects of their lives. The insights offered here in terms of the context will provide design researchers with a better understanding of these and the opportunities for research as a result. The chapter has addressed several different challenges related to diagnosis, care, quality of life, ethics as well as the different contexts where research in dementia is targeted, such as the home, nursing home, hospital and community.

References

Alsaeed, D., Jamieson, E., Gul, M. O. and Smith, F. J. (2016). Challenges to optimal medicines use in people living with dementia and their caregivers: a literature review. *International Journal of Pharmaceutics*, 512 (2): 396–404.

All-Party Parliamentary Group on Dementia (APPG). (2016). *Dementia Rarely Travels Alone: Living with Dementia and Other Conditions*. London: Alzheimer's Society.

Bartlett, R., Milne, R. and Croucher, R. (2018). Strategies to improve recruitment of people with dementia to research studies. *Dementia*, 1471301217748503.

Brodaty, H. and Donkin, M. (2009). Family caregivers of people with dementia. *Dialogues in Clinical Neuroscience*, 11 (2): 217.

Brumback-Peltz, C., Balasubramanian, A. B., Corrada, M. M. and Kawas, C. H. (2011). Diagnosing dementia in the oldest-old. *Maturitas*, 70 (2): 164–168.

Chang, E., Daly, J., Johnson, A., Harrison, K., Easterbrook, S., Bidewell, J. ... and Hancock, K. (2009). Challenges for professional care of advanced dementia. *International Journal of Nursing Practice*, 15 (1): 41–47.

Chaudhury, H., and Cooke, H. (2014). Design matters in dementia care: the role of the physical environment in dementia care settings. *Excellence in Dementia Care*, 2, 144–158.

Chen, S., Boyle, L. L., Conwell, Y., Xiao, S., and Chiu, H. F. K. (2014). The challenges of dementia care in rural China. *International Psychogeriatrics*, 26 (7): 1059–1064.

Connell, C. M., Janevic, M. R., and Gallant, M. P. (2001). The costs of caring: impact of dementia on family caregivers. *Journal of Geriatric Psychiatry and Neurology*, 14 (4): 179–187.

Dewing, J. (2007). Participatory research: a method for process consent with persons who have dementia. *Dementia*, 6 (1): 11–25.

Ekström, A., Ferm, U. and Samuelsson, C. (2017). Digital communication support and Alzheimer's disease. *Dementia*, 16 (6): 711–731.

Førsund, L. H., Grov, E. K., Helvik, A. S., Juvet, L. K., Skovdahl, K. and Eriksen, S. (2018). The experience of lived space in persons with dementia: a systematic meta-synthesis. *BMC Geriatrics*, 18 (1): 33.

George, J., Long, S. and Vincent, C. (2013). How can we keep patients with dementia safe in our acute hospitals? A review of challenges and solutions. *Journal of the Royal Society of Medicine*, 106 (9): 355–361.

Gray, K., Evans, S. C., Griffiths, A. and Schneider, J. (2017). Critical reflections on methodological challenge in arts and dementia evaluation and research. *Dementia*, 1471301217734478.

Greenwood, N. and Smith, R. (2016). The experiences of people with young-onset dementia: a meta-ethnographic review of the qualitative literature. *Maturitas*, 92, 102–109.

Grill, J. D., Raman, R., Ernstrom, K., Aisen, P. and Karlawish, J. (2013). Effect of study partner on the conduct of Alzheimer disease clinical trials. *Neurology*, 80 (3): 282–288.

Hubbard, G., Downs, M. G. and Tester, S. (2003). Including older people with dementia in research: challenges and strategies. *Aging and Mental Health*, 7 (5): 351–362.

Johannessen, A. and Möller, A. (2013). Experiences of persons with early-onset dementia in everyday life: a qualitative study. *Dementia*, 12 (4): 410–424.

Jones, D. (2015). A family living with Alzheimer's disease: the communicative challenges. *Dementia*, 14 (5): 555–573.

Koo, M-Y, Pusey, H. and Keady, J. (2020). 'I try my best … I try to relieve the burden of my mum': a narrative analysis of the everyday caregiving experiences for five intergenerational Singapore-Chinese families where one member has a dementia. *Ageing & Society*, available online first at: doi: 10.1017/S0144686X20000070.

Lambert, M. A., Bickel, H., Prince, M., Fratiglioni, L., Von Strauss, E., Frydecka, D., Kiejna, A., Georges, J. and Reynish, E. L. (2014). Estimating the burden of early onset dementia; systematic review of disease prevalence. *European Journal of Neurology*, 21 (4): 563–569.

Lynn, J. D., Rondón-Sulbarán, J., Quinn, E., Ryan, A., McCormack, B. and Martin, S. (2019). A systematic review of electronic assistive technology within supporting living environments for people with dementia. *Dementia*, 18 (7–8): 2371–2435.

McKeown, J., Clarke, A., Ingleton, C. and Repper, J. (2010). Actively involving people with dementia in qualitative research. *Journal of Clinical Nursing*, 19 (13–14): 1935–1943.

Moore, T. F. and Hollett, J. (2003). Giving voice to persons living with dementia: the researcher's opportunities and challenges. *Nursing Science Quarterly*, 16 (2): 163–167.

Moyle, W. and Murfield, J. E. (2013). Health-related quality of life in older people with severe dementia: challenges for measurement and management. *Expert Review of Pharmacoeconomics & Outcomes Research*, 13 (1): 109–122.

Nehen, H. G. and Hermann, D. M. (2015). Supporting dementia patients and their caregivers in daily life challenges: review of physical, cognitive and psychosocial intervention studies. *European Journal of Neurology*, 22 (2): 246-e20.

Niemeijer, A. R., Depla, M. F., Frederiks, B. J. and Hertogh, C. M. (2015). The experiences of people with dementia and intellectual disabilities with surveillance technologies in residential care. *Nursing Ethics*, 22 (3): 307–320.

Nygård, L. (2004). Responses of persons with dementia to challenges in daily activities: a synthesis of findings from empirical studies. *American Journal of Occupational Therapy*, 58 (4): 435–445.

Nygård, L. (2008). The meaning of everyday technology as experienced by people with dementia who live alone. *Dementia*, 7 (4): 481–502.

Pesonen, H. M., Remes, A. M. and Isola, A. (2011). Ethical aspects of researching subjective experiences in early-stage dementia. *Nursing Ethics*, 18 (5): 651–661.

Phinney, A. and Moody, E. M. (2011). Leisure connections: benefits and challenges of participating in a social recreation group for people with early dementia. *Activities, Adaptation & Aging*, 35 (2): 111–130.

Phinney, A., Chaudhury, H. and O'Connor, D. L. (2007). Doing as much as I can do: the meaning of activity for people with dementia. *Aging and Mental Health*, 11 (4): 384–393.

Poblador-Plou, B., Calderón-Larrañaga, A., Marta-Moreno, J., Hancco-Saavedra, J., Sicras-Mainar, A., Soljak, M. and Prados-Torres, A. (2014). Comorbidity of dementia: a cross-sectional study of primary care older patients. *BMC Psychiatry*, 14 (1): 84.

Prince, M., Comas-Herrera, A., Knapp, M., Guerchet, M. and Karagiannidou, M. (2016). World Alzheimer report 2016: improving healthcare for people living with dementia: coverage, quality and costs now and in the future. London: Alzheimer's Disease International (ADI).

Roach, P., Drummond, N. and Keady, J. (2016). 'Nobody would say that it is Alzheimer's or dementia at this age': family adjustment following a diagnosis of early-onset dementia. *Journal of Aging Studies*, 36, 26–32.

Rossor, M. N., Fox, N. C., Mummery, C. J., Schott, J. M. and Warren, J. D. (2010). The diagnosis of young-onset dementia. *The Lancet Neurology*, 9 (8): 793–806.

Samsi, K., Abley, C., Campbell, S., Keady, J., Manthorpe, J., Robinson, L., Watts, S. and Bond, J. (2014). Negotiating a Labyrinth: experiences of assessment and diagnostic journey in cognitive impairment and dementia. *International Journal of Geriatric Psychiatry*, 29 (1): 58–67

Scrutton, J. and Brancati, C. U. (2016). *Dementia and Comorbidities: Ensuring Parity of Care*. London: ILC.

Sherratt, C., Soteriou, T. and Evans, S. (2007). Ethical issues in social research involving people with dementia. *Dementia*, 6 (4): 463–479.

Silva, P., Kergoat, M. J. and Shatenstein, B. (2013). Challenges in managing the diet of older adults with early-stage Alzheimer dementia: a caregiver perspective. *The Journal of Nutrition, Health & Aging*, 17 (2): 142–147.

Slavin, M. J., Brodaty, H. and Sachdev, P. S. (2013). Challenges of diagnosing dementia in the oldest old population. *Journals of Gerontology Series A: Biomedical Sciences and Medical Sciences*, 68 (9): 1103–1111

Soilemezi, D., Drahota, A., Crossland, J. and Stores, R. (2017). The role of the home environment in dementia care and support: systematic review of qualitative research. *Dementia*, 1471301217692130.

Thuné-Boyle, I. C., Sampson, E. L., Jones, L., King, M., Lee, D. R. and Blanchard, M. R. (2010). Challenges to improving end of life care of people with advanced dementia in the UK. *Dementia*, 9 (2): 259–284.

Wang, J., Xiao, L. D., He, G. P. and De Bellis, A. (2014). Family caregiver challenges in dementia care in a country with undeveloped dementia services. *Journal of Advanced Nursing*, 70 (6): 1369–1380.

Wolverson, E. L., Clarke, C. and Moniz-Cook, E. (2010). Remaining hopeful in early-stage dementia: a qualitative study. *Aging and Mental Health*, 14 (4): 450–460.

Xiao, L. D., Wang, J., He, G. P., De Bellis, A., Verbeeck, J. and Kyriazopoulos, H. (2014). Family caregiver challenges in dementia care in Australia and China: a critical perspective. *BMC Geriatrics*, 14 (1): 6.

Zarit, S. H. and Femia, E. E. (2008). A future for family care and dementia intervention research? Challenges and strategies. *Aging and Mental Health*, 12 (1): 5–13.

4 Material
Design research methods and applications

Introduction

This chapter will provide the reader with an understanding about the different design research methods that can actively be used to both support and empower people living with dementia. Whilst this is not a textbook on research methodology, it is important that we briefly cover some of the main ontological and epistemological foundations of research in order to provide a context for the focus on design research methods. This will include an appreciation about the foundations and language of research. However, in adhering to the underpinning vision and values of this book, the primary focus of this chapter will be on outlining participatory approaches to research and the importance of co-design and co-production alongside people living with dementia. This will be expressed through patient and public involvement in research and we will pay particular attention as to how people living with dementia might want to be positioned in the research process, from setting the research question to taking part in dissemination activities. We will illustrate this involvement through reference to the COINED model (Swarbrick et al., 2019). This focus will point a direction towards a more egalitarian and democratised approach to undertaking and evaluating design research. The chapter will conclude with two brief examples of relevant work where design research methods have been used and applied in the dementia studies field.

The foundations and language of research: An overview

Over a decade ago, and after assimilating the literature available at the time, Watson and Keady (2008) provided a straightforward definition of research, namely: 'research is systematic and aims to create new knowledge or verify existing knowledge' (p. 7). This definition would suggest that the purpose of research is to generate knowledge and insights about the world in which we live. However, the nature of the research inquiry will vary depending upon the stance that is taken to view the world and how 'truth' is understood – either as universal or context-specific. For example, if the world around us is seen as being 'external and fixed' then to generate and test theory based on this belief structure, quantitative (also known as experimental) research designs will be used to measure representations of universal truth. On the other hand, if the world is viewed as 'fluid and plural' then qualitative approaches will be used to represent/generate theory within a version of the 'truth' that is context-specific. In other words, the search for the 'truth' in qualitative research is located within a meaning that the event has for the person him- or herself and how reality is then constructed from a subjective perspective.

At their most basic level, randomised controlled trials are used to establish the existence of a fixed (universal) truth and this is operationalised through the generation and testing of hypothesis. In quantitative research design, object-ivity and distance are the watchwords of theory production. The research question and theory are generated by the researcher/research team by a pro-cess of logical deduction, such as by using the findings of previous studies or systematic reviews. Samples of similar characteristics are then recruited into the study and divided (blindly) into either an experimental or a control group, ideally of similar numbers. It will be the experimental group that receives the intervention whilst the control group that will continue to receive 'treatment' as usual. Before and after measures are then agreed and a primary outcome measure selected. Bias is removed in the study design and nowadays, in the UK at least, this is most often undertaken by an independent Clinical Trials Unit. This independent role is to ensure that the intervention (which could, of course, be a design intervention) that is being introduced to the experimental group is conducted in a randomised, rigorous and blind manner. The impact of the introduced intervention is then measured objectively and compared across and between groups. When compared to the control group, and using the same primary outcome measure, if the intervention introduced into the experimental group is seen to be effective through a statistical power calcula-tion – and the sampling strategy is large enough – then this would represent a universal 'truth' that is replicable in all similar situations.

Randomised controlled trials are often positioned as the highest form of evidence and along with systematic reviews, especially Cochrane Reviews, as the apex of scientific knowledge generation (Hassan et al., 2016). In addition to experimental and control groups, and the introduction of an intervention, the language of the experimental design will include such terminology as: pla-cebo effects, blind techniques (e.g. single-blind and double-blind techniques), cluster randomisation, quasi-experimental design, pre-test-post-test experi-mental design and the Hawthorne effect. In the space we have in this chapter, it is simply not possible to outline all the meanings attached to the set of descriptions. Therefore, for interested readers, a list of more substantive textbooks and resources on research methodology and design is included in the 'additional reading' list supplied at the end of this chapter. However, it is suffice to say, in the dementia studies field, and leaving to one side the debate on how effective the primary outcome measures are in measuring the needs of people living with dementia (see: Reilly et al., 2020), the power and influence of the randomised controlled trial can be seen in the presentation of 'best practice evidence' included in the most recent National Institute for Health and Care Excellence (NICE) dementia guideline (NICE, 2018; nice. org.uk/guidance/ng97; accessed 24 July 2020). Interestingly, in the presentation of the NICE dementia guideline, an absence of effective psychosocial interventions in dementia is highlighted, especially in communication and other psychosocial interventions (for an illustration see: Woods et al., 2016) and representations of the effectiveness of design interventions are limited.

In contrast to quantitative research, qualitative research approaches, such as phenomenology, grounded theory, interpretive phenomenological analysis, narrative research, case study, cooperative inquiry and ethnography, whilst differing in their ontology and epistemology, are held together by a representation of human experience that is grounded in the individual and in their subjective interpretation of events and the meaning that it holds. Moreover, all qualitative research approaches use similar methods, such as interviews (unstructured/semi-structured/structured/walking), video-elicitation and observation techniques, but *how* they are used and *why* they are being used may differ between approaches. This will also be the case with the approach to data analysis attached to the methodology, such as reflexive thematic analysis (Braun and Clarke, 2019) for ethnographic research or constant comparative analysis in grounded theory (Glaser and Strauss, 1967; Glaser, 1978). However, whatever analytical approach is followed, theory in qualitative research is produced that reflects the experiences of the sample recruited into the study, rather than making claims of universal truth, and relies on the reflexivity of the researcher as an instrument of the research process (Foley, 2002; May and Perry, 2017). As a note of caution, that analysis itself is an over-simplification as the original design of grounded theory (Glaser and Strauss, 1967) made the claim of developing testable qualitative research. For example, the central ideas and philosophy shared in Glaser and Strauss' (1967) seminal text '*The Discovery of Grounded Theory: Strategies for Qualitative Research*' stated that grounded theories seek to explain and predict phenomena under study and to build mid-range theory. This was evident in the development of constant comparative analysis, which Glaser and Strauss (1967) saw as a general approach 'just as statistics exist for the experimental methods' (p. 21). The authors added the addendum that both approaches use the logic of comparison and are thereby 'equal' in their predictive qualities.

Whilst there is so much to admire in the work of Glaser and Strauss (1967), and their later publications (Glaser, 1978; Strauss and Corbin, 1990; Glaser, 1992), at the turn of the millennium Kathy Charmaz (2000) put forward the notion of 'constructivist grounded theory' to try to wrestle control of data collection and analysis away from the researcher and into the hands of the person being researched (see also: Charmaz, 2006). Charmaz (2000) termed this shift of emphasis the 'mutual creation of knowledge by the viewer and viewed' (p. 510) and believed that a more authentic grounded theory study would emerge if participants were encouraged/empowered to 'cast their stories in their terms' (p. 525). This more participatory way of doing research, be that through constructivist grounded theory or other emancipatory designs and approaches, such as participatory action research (Morgan et al., 2014), will shortly be developed further.

However, before leaving this opening section, we would like to highlight two further issues. Firstly, there is a movement towards mixed methods research, which is a combination of both quantitative and qualitative approaches. This inter-relationship between the two research paradigms can be seen in the most recent (2019) version of the MRC Framework for Developing and Evaluating Complex Interventions (https://mrc.ukri.org/documents/pdf/complex-interventions-guidance/; accessed 20 July 2020) where exploratory, qualitative work in the early phases of the research process helps to guide and inform the intervention and evaluation that subsequently follows. The work by Windle et al. (2016) on dementia and arts intervention is a good example of such a blending of knowledge and science bases in mixed methods research. Secondly, there is also a movement to see the importance of practice knowledge in the development of research that is undertaken on the frontline by experienced clinicians. This could be especially important in design research when designers themselves hold positions which interact on a regular basis with members of the public or patients, which in our case and in the context of this book, we are operationalising as people living with dementia. Stemming directly from the work of Reed and Procter (1995) and their stance on practitioner-research, Sally Thorne's (2008) book entitled *Interpretive Description* seeks to balance this practice and research knowledge and acknowledge that both approaches have rewards and limitations. This is perhaps best seen in Thorne's (2008) definition of the approach:

> Interpretive description is a qualitative research approach that requires an integrity of purpose deriving from two sources: 1) an actual practice goal, and 2) an understanding of what we do and don't know on the basis of the available empirical evidence (from all sources).
>
> (p. 35)

As the above outline demonstrates, this push to generate new insights extends to the development of a literature review which is usually one of the first steps on a research process to establish the nature of the research question and its underpinning aims and objectives. In interpretive description, Thorne (2008) defines this as 'scaffolding a study' and puts an emphasis on the 'researcher' being able to bring their own positionality and subjective experiences to the review findings. It is an interesting angle on developing research and one which may be of benefit to experienced designers working alongside people living with dementia.

Participatory approaches

In the UK, the National Institute for Health Research (NIHR) have helped to support the development of INVOLVE which is about finding new ways of doing research and involving members of the public in all aspects of research practice. As INVOLVE (2012) have described, participatory approaches to research are carried out 'with' or 'by' members of the public rather than 'to', 'about' or 'for' them. Indeed, Professor Dame Sally Davies, who was the Chief Medical Officer in the UK in 2009, wrote the following clarifying statement about the important of participatory approaches in a contemporaneous report:

> No matter how complicated the research, or how brilliant the researcher, patients and the public always offer unique, invaluable insights. Their advice when designing, implementing and evaluating research invariably makes studies more effective, more credible and often more cost efficient as well.
>
> (Davies, Foreword in Staley, 2009)

There is no doubt that this is an important challenge and direction, but it is not a new one. As Northway (2008) previously identified, the origins of participatory research stem from Tanzania in the late 1970s and the first meeting of the International Participatory Research Network. At this meeting, the network produced a definition of participatory research and emphasised a focus on promoting the active participation of powerless groups at all stages of the research process (for additional information see: Hall and Kidd, 1978). From the very outset, countering oppression of disenfranchised groups was an important goal of participatory research and this standpoint remains an inherent value base of the approach. By giving a voice to the voiceless, the sociological and political dimensions of participatory research should not be forgotten or under-estimated when setting out to conduct such work.

Williams and Keady (2021) have recently argued that from these early roots of participatory research to the present day, three threads of inquiry have unified the approach. Firstly, social investigation that engages ordinary people. Secondly, an educational process based on interaction between researchers and participants. Thirdly, researchers being in solidarity with people to take collective action. Accordingly, participatory research has been influenced by a range of movements and writings, including the work of Paulo Freire a Brazilian educator and philosopher whose writings emanated from the critique that social science, education and developmental work may exacerbate the position of people as being oppressed, or dominated, rather than contribute to their liberation as citizens (Freire, 1970; Maguire, 1987). That said, the tradition of participatory research work is both well established and diverse within the qualitative tradition.

Commenting on this shift of power from the researcher to community control, Stoecker (1999, p. 850) identified six key points where decisions are needed to be made:

- Defining the research question
- Designing the research

- Implementing the research design
- Analysing the research data
- Reporting the research results
- Acting on the research results

Participatory research has therefore become increasingly prominent as it seeks to provide the vulnerable with a 'voice' in the health and social sciences, engaging them and researchers in emancipatory methods (Aldridge, 2015). An overarching boundary set by Reason (1994) and Freire (1970) was that at its core, participatory research was emancipatory, action-orientated and participatory. It is to a consideration of these issues as they intersect with, and impact upon, people living with dementia that we will now consider. To do that, we will draw upon the work of Swarbrick et al. (2019) where one of the book authors, John Keady, was a co-author on the article. The section is shared with the permission of the publisher as acknowledged at the end of this chapter.

Participatory design is a recognised approach (Simonsen and Robertson, 2012) to include people with lived experience in decision-making processes that affect their lives. Participatory design has its roots in Europe where labour unions raised the public awareness of the interrelation between technology in the workplace and its social effects (Muller and Kuhn, 1993; Simonsen and Robertson, 2012). It originated in Scandinavia in the late 1960s as workers pushed for input into the design of technology being introduced into their workplaces (Schuler and Namioka, 1993). The approach involves the inter-action of stakeholders at all stages of the design process. Participatory design takes into account the perceptions and experiences of people living with dementia and their caregivers and other stakeholder group, involves research beneficiaries not merely as research subjects, but as co-researchers in studying the issues at hand and as co-designers in developing creative solutions. Researchers have already started to explore participatory design within the context of dementia research and developing ways for employing participa-tory design methods with people living with dementia (Hwang et al., 2012; Lindsay et al., 2012; Span et al., 2018; Hendriks et al., 2018).

Involving people living with dementia in research

As we have seen, over the last decade or so within the UK, research funding councils and charities have demanded greater transparency from academic bidding teams to demonstrate how people with lived experience (of the proposed topic under study) have been, or will be, involved in the research process (see for example: Iliffe et al., 2013; Frank et al., 2020). Involvement may range from mapping out how people with lived experience have been involved in proposal development to a detailed consideration about future plans for the person's involvement in data collection, data analysis and pro-ject dissemination. This is often referred to as Patient and Public Involvement, or PPI for short. Indeed, nowadays, it is not uncommon for those with the lived experience of dementia to be integral members of academic bidding teams in order to demonstrate an authentic commitment to PPI engagement. Wright et al. (2010) viewed such partnerships as a 'core component of good research practice' (p. 359) and they speak to the vision of PPI engagement as highlighted earlier by Professor Dame Sally Davies.

Set against these key messages, developments within the PPI arena is increasingly important in the field of dementia studies (Harris and Sterin, 1999; Tanner, 2012; Litherland et al., 2018; Burton et al., 2019), albeit at a slow rate (Bethell et al., 2018) and a need to continually involve people living with dementia in all planning and participatory steps (Swaffer, 2016). For example, Alzheimer Europe (2011) set out their principles of research encouraging a change in ideology from research 'on' people living with dementia to research 'alongside' or 'with' people living with dementia. Building on this foundation, the Scottish Dementia Working Group and The University of Edinburgh (2013) developed their own core principles for involving people living with dementia in research, such as 'we want to be valued, and to be kept involved and informed' (core principle 1) and 'we are often involved in answering research questions, but we are not often asked about research priorities' (core principle 2). This change in direction has also entered the UK political discourse through the first Prime Minister's challenge on dementia (Department of Health, 2012, p. 5), which identified three national policy drivers and key commitments: (i) driving improvements in health and care; (ii) creating dementia friendly communities that understand how to help and (iii) better research. This inclusive agenda recognised the citizenship of people living with dementia (Bartlett and O'Connor, 2010; Dröes et al., 2017) and was further endorsed through the Prime Minister's second challenge on dementia (Department of Health, 2015) which highlighted the partnership in dementia research between 'patients, researchers, funders and society' (p. 46).

However, despite this high-profile association, research involving people living dementia positioned as authentic co-researchers is still in its formative stages (Miah et al., 2019). The primary reason for this positioning is fourfold. Firstly, people living with dementia have traditionally been seen as either a 'subject' or 'participant'. Secondly, there have been a lack of opportunities for people living with dementia to be involved and engaged in research. Thirdly, the time-consuming and legislative requirements of establishing capacity, obtaining consent and safeguarding anonymity in the research process. Fourthly, the difficulty in obtaining ethical approval for studies when people living with dementia transition from being a 'participant' in a study to the role of 'co-researcher' (see for example: Clarke et al., 2018; Webb et al., 2020). For ethical committees, balancing the judgement of capacity and the politics of anonymity are difficult constructs (and responsibilities) to resolve and further work is necessary to help provide clarity to the field. As McKeown et al. (2010), Higgins (2013) and Waite et al. (2019) have all contended, such obstacles are barriers for people living with dementia's inclusivity and full citizenship in society.

To try and respond to this dilemma, we will now outline the development of the 'CO-researcher INvolvement and Engagement in Dementia' Model, or the COINED model for short. The COINED model is presented in this chapter as a guide for design researchers to continue to build a co-design and co-research programme of work based around its shared themes, each of which have been developed alongside people living with dementia and took a number of years to develop.

Introducing the COINED model

Context

The COINED model was initially developed during the application stage of the subsequently funded Neighbourhoods and Dementia Study (2014–2019), which was a large, multi-centre, international and mixed methods study (see: Keady et al., 2014; and also: https://sites.manchester.ac.uk/neighbourhoods-and-dementia/; accessed 24 July 2020). One of the book's co-authors, John Keady, was the Chief Investigator to this five-year programme of work. Funded jointly by the Economic and Social Research Council (ESRC) and the NIHR under action point 12 of the first Prime Minister's challenge on dementia (Department of Health, 2012), the Neighbourhoods and Dementia Study (the Neighbourhoods study hereafter) comprised eight work programmes where the central aims were to: centralise the vision and values of people living with dementia and their carer partners in research practice; embrace creativity, innovation and shared stories; and empower the experience of people living with dementia, their care partners and neighbourhood networks. Work programme 1 of the Neighbourhoods study was entitled 'Member Involvement' and it is from where the COINED model was developed. Facilitated by Caroline Swarbrick, work programme 1 had a dual aim. Firstly, to facilitate the involvement of people living with dementia in all of the work programmes as co-researchers on the Neighbourhoods study; and secondly, to support people living with dementia to co-design and lead neighbourhoods-focused research projects. In all work on the Neighbourhoods study, the descriptive term 'co-researcher' was adopted to reflect a desire to move away from references to 'user' and 'patient and public involvement' and head towards a more collaborative partnership between groups of people living with dementia (acting as co-researchers), academic co-researchers, service providers and society as a whole.

Methods

A number of peer-peer activist groups of people living with dementia located in the UK were involved in the development of the COINED model over a three-year cycle. These were: Open Doors, located in Salford, Greater Manchester; EDUCATE (the Early Dementia Users Co-operative Aiming To Educate), based in Stockport, Greater Manchester; and the Scottish Dementia Working Group (based in Scotland). Facilitated by Caroline Swarbrick positioned as the academic co-researcher, all groups led on the development of the COINED model. The groups met independently with Caroline acting as a conduit for the exchange of ideas and thoughts. Whilst this was theoretically a 'PPI' activity, the principles of participatory action research (Morgan et al., 2014) were adopted, with a focus on 'collaborative, equitable partnership in all phases of the research' (Blair and Minkler, 2009, p. 653).

Using INVOLVE's generic research cycle (INVOLVE, 2012, p. 25) as a starting point, the remit of discussions was to identify ways in which members of the groups would like to be involved as co-researchers across the research trajectory which the groups defined as: (i) supporting us; (ii) identifying research opportunities; (iii) designing the research; (iv) collecting data; (v) the findings; (vi) getting the results 'out there'. Framed around these steps, group members next developed a more comprehensive compendium of themes of co-researcher involvement and engagement in research which is shown in Figure 4.1.

Each component of the COINED model represents inclusivity, mutual respect and empowerment. Figure 4.1 can be read as starting at 'Ongoing consultation' and then moving clockwise around the diagram, so next reaching

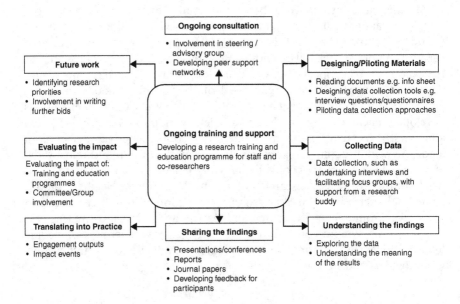

Figure 4.1 The CO-researcher INvolvement and Engagement in Dementia (COINED) model.

Source: Swarbrick et al. (2019). Figure reproduced with the kind permission of the publisher.

the theme heading 'Designing/Piloting materials' and then on through to 'Future work'. Each theme heading has a set of bullet points positioned under it so that additional information is provided as to what people living with dementia expect from taking part under each theme. In looking at the contents of each theme heading in Figure 4.1, there is no expectation that people living with dementia would travel around the diagram. So, if the person living with dementia wanted to stop at 'Ongoing consultation' and felt comfortable in that activity, then no additional expectations would be put in place to move on to the next theme heading. As such, the headings and activities named in the COINED model move at a pace that the person living with dementia feels most comfortable with.

At its centre, and underpinning the COINED model, is 'on-going training and support' (for co-researchers). Swarbrick et al. (2019) recommend that such support should be provided for the duration of the research process. Group members were insistent that support should be provided from an academic standpoint in parallel to peer support, either through formal agencies (including dementia support organisations, such as the Alzheimer's Society) or informal peer support network. The voice of people living with dementia is principal to the mode of inquiry as 'experts by experience' with representation embedded as a continuous presence throughout the research process, as defined in Figure 4.1. In addition, the importance of peer support in providing a community network was highlighted as being essential in order to maintain the person living with dementia's well-being, self-confidence and a sense of security within an ever-changing environment and relationship to the world.

In the original participatory action research design that led to the development of the COINED model (Swarbrick et al., 2019), discussion focused on the collection and analysis of data, and more specifically around the level of objectivity expected by the co-researcher, and the extent to which someone with the lived experience of dementia was able to deliver that objectivity. Group members acknowledged the potential risk that the co-researcher may influence the responses given by the participant by sharing their own experiences, inadvertently extending their own peer support discourse. Paradoxically, group members were also aware that shared experiences (between the co-researcher and participant living with dementia) has the potential to enrich the responses given. On balance, group members were aware that the data collected by a co-researcher (as a person living with dementia) would inevitably provide different levels of richness, depth and context compared to data collected by an academic co-researcher.

In the development of the COINED model, exploring the data and understanding the meaning of the results were key discussion points, whereby disparity between the collection of data, its presentation in the final report and the lack of transparency was noted as devaluing the role of people living with dementia in research (both as co-researchers and as participants). 'Accessibility' featured at the very heart of effective communication, particularly in terms of language and terminology used. Indeed, using a cooperative inquiry design (Heron, 1996), a later sub-set of the Open Doors research team went on to develop a set of language guidance for use in any dementia-related outputs or publications (see: Swarbrick et al., 2020). As this information was not available at the time of developing the COINED model, some of the main outcomes of this work and language guidance are highlighted in Table 4.1.

Table 4.1 Language guidance for use in any dementia-related outputs or publication

---

When writing about 'dementia'
  Terms to use:
  • Dementia
  • Symptoms of dementia
  • Younger onset dementia

  Terms to avoid:
  • Senile/senility
  • Slang expressions of dementia
  • Early onset dementia
  • Disease

When writing about 'behaviour'
  Terms to use:
  • Changed behaviours
  • Expressions of unmet need
  • Behavioural and psychological symptoms of dementia (only when used in a clinical setting)

  Terms to avoid:
  • Challenging behaviours
  • Difficult behaviours
  • Behaviours of concern

When writing about 'people'
  Terms to use:
  • Person with dementia
  • Person living with dementia
  • Person supporting someone living with dementia
  • Living with/caring for/supporting a person who has dementia
  • Effect / impact of supporting someone with dementia

  Terms to avoid:
  • Demented/dementing
  • Sufferer/suffering
  • Subject
  • Patient (unless in a clinical context)
  • Service User
  • Client
  • Victim
  • Abbreviations, such as PWD
  • Carer burden

The co-research team recommended that all written text should be presented in Arial font no smaller than size pt14

Source: Adapted from Swarbrick et al. (2020).

In operationalising the COINED model, knowledge exchange was regarded as fundamental to the advancement of learning for all. There was also a general feeling that the process of translating research into practice was often disparate and fragmented. Subsequently, group members advocated the involvement of people living with dementia in presenting research findings alongside academic co-researchers in ways which would be creative, accessible and meaningful to all.

In the Neighbourhoods study, several members of the Member Involvement groups, who also had an academic background, raised the issue of 'impact'. Given the different meanings and interpretations of the term, the authorship agreed that in the context of the COINED model, that the term 'impact' would be used to refer to the effectiveness of the research or the effectiveness of the involvement of people living with dementia as co-researchers. Discussions also extended to the narrative of 'evaluation' that was regarded as an integral mechanism of the research in 'measuring' impact. This discussion was necessary to ensure that people living with dementia acting as co-researchers were 'getting it right' (see Figure 4.1). It was felt that the processes and outcomes of any evaluation would be crucial to the group's learning and needed to be embedded within further decision-making. Thus, in the vision and values inherent in the COINED model, it was anticipated that learning from the research findings would help to identify, shape and frame further research priorities. As reported by Swarbrick et al. (2019), group members were seen to appreciate the ongoing shift in research priorities to meet the needs of the changing landscape of dementia care and fluctuating needs of people living with dementia. Indeed, as seen in Figure 4.1, involvement in future work was regarded as pivotal in positioning people living with dementia at the centre of research in the context of collaboration and focus. Meeting such needs is an on-going challenge for all social science researchers involved in research activities, including design researchers.

Two examples of design research studies in dementia

Over the years, researchers working in the design and the lived experience of dementia space have used a diverse range of methods and methodological approaches to underpin their work and its reporting. In this section, we will draw on the writing that has been shared in this chapter to bring to life some of its underpinning concepts and ideas. To do this, we will briefly outline two examples of published studies in the design research field and in study 2 (below), we will specifically highlight the importance of participatory methods to enhance co-design and co-production by working alongside people living with dementia – in this case people with more advanced dementia – as an approach to enhance the authenticity of research reporting.

Design research study 1

Article reference:
Gareth Chalfont. 2007. Wholistic design in dementia care. *Journal of Housing for the Elderly*, 21 (1/2): 153–177.

What the article covered

This study explored the design of a person living with dementia's connection to nature within care homes. It was an exploratory qualitative design that led to the design and description of six domains: Person; Location; Architecture; Nature; Energy; and Technology. These domains were abbreviated to PLANET in the article and it proposed that these domains were used as a comprehensive checklist for investigating the potential for connection to nature for people living with dementia living in care environments. The research reported in the article was conducted between 2001 and 2003 with residents living with dementia and carers in two separate assisted living facilities in the USA, a specialist home for people living with dementia in Scandinavia and two residential care homes in the UK. The article used: a variety of floorplan diagrams to give an idea about space and the person living with dementia relationship to their environment; a number of photographs to reveal how people with dementia were living in the care environment, such as a view from a resident's bedroom to the care home garden; and a selection of quotes from interaction between the author and the resident living with dementia, who is given anonymity through the alignment of a numerical code (e.g. R1 for resident living with dementia). In addition to the main focus of the paper on PLANET and how each of the domains can be developed (e.g. under Architecture it was possible to record that a shed existed on site), the article gave an interesting insight into the importance of nature acting as a stimulus for conversation. The importance of edge spaces in the everyday lives of residents was raised with edge spaces acting as a conduit for the person living with dementia's connection to nature.

Design research study 2

Article reference:
Gail Kenning. 2018. Reciprocal design: inclusive design approaches for people with late stage dementia. *Design for Health*, 2 (1): 142–162.

What the article covered

Emanating from Australia, this study focussed on the importance of designers gaining a holistic understanding into the embodied experience of living with dementia and the importance of participatory work alongside people living with dementia – and that such connection was meaningful for all participants.

The design research project used an interpretivist approach drawing on social and reflexive approaches to understand how to co-design objects and activities for people living with dementia while also providing opportunities for social interaction and engagement during the design process. The study used three levels of engagement in the design research project, i) workshop participants including people living with dementia and stakeholders in their care, such as family members, carers, care staff and management from the care provider organisation; ii) design researchers experienced in design and research methodologies (including the author) who also collected and analysed data and were involved in the production of prototypes alongside the designers; and iii) designers, with experience in product design, textiles, industrial design and art and technology and who 'worked at a distance from the workshop participants', but engaged directly with the design researchers as they all developed prototypes that were explored and developed in subsequent workshops. The article contained a series of colour photographs that showed the workshop groups in action and they were carefully staged so as not to reveal the identity of any of the people living with dementia taking part. By following the research design, the article was able to share a range of prototypes that came out of the time together, such as a 'Fashion Studio Kit' that enabled fashion outfits to be assembled from a range of miniature clothing items made from fabrics and threads; 'Fiddle Blankets' with pompoms, beads or buttons to be grasped and touched; 'Fiddle Cushions' made from a range of fabrics with buttons, beads and similar attachments and a 'Flower Arranging Kit' with magnetic fabric flowers that could be arranged to make a picture. Importantly, the author revealed that not all participants living with dementia were able to envisage the design project as a whole or their part in the design process or 'future think' end outcomes. The project therefore focused on the concept of reciprocity in design research.

Discussion

As Kenning (2018) has reported, design has an important role to play in supporting quality of life of people living with dementia and that co-creative approaches can enable people living with dementia and other care partners to engage in the design process and impact products and services made for them. As Kenning (2018) goes on to explain, such opportunities are important as they facilitate social engagement, interaction and pleasure, and 'give designers insights into the embodied experience of living with dementia and the social and cultural impact' (p. 142). However, going forward, one of the challenges is to continue to develop and instil a participatory ethos in the research process. As we have discussed in this chapter, the involvement of people living with dementia as co-researchers and co-designers is not without its challenges and ethical debates. Particularly within the remit of data collection, analysis and dissemination (see Figure 4.1), anonymity (or otherwise) and participant confidentiality (or otherwise). Whilst academic researchers are bound by the

UK Policy Framework for Health and Social Care Research (Department of Health, 2020), and its 15 principles of good practice that range from 'safety' through to 'compliance', to the best of our knowledge there are no parallel frameworks for co-researchers which would, of course, address the needs of people living with dementia. As such, there is a space and a vacuum in research practices that is yet to be filled. Accordingly, there is a need to formalise the expectations and responsibilities of co-researchers, especially when set against the challenges of co-design research and the ambition of the field to provide the highest quality evidence and standards from which to build new directions.

Whilst discussions in the wider literature focus on whether people living with dementia as co-researchers are able to engage in ways that are 'meaningful' to the research process (Tanner, 2012), the approach in the COINED model is to ensure that co-researcher involvement is, first and foremost, meaningful for the individuals themselves, thus respecting and empowering the personhood of people living with dementia (Kitwood, 1997). One of the key messages of the COINED model is to ensure that its implementation allows for creative methods and expressive output and should not be constrained by traditional research methods and processes. So, for instance, the use of animation to storyboard lives became one of the research outputs and directions organised by people living with dementia taking part in the Neighbourhoods study and trying to explain the impact that stigma had on daily living (Davis, 2020). This is important as visual and sensory methods appear to be favoured by people living with dementia in the 'doing' of research – this was also a focus in the description of design research study 2 by Kenning (2018). Therefore, design researchers may well have to adapt their methods to the ones best understood by people living with dementia and start to implement emancipatory research methodologies to connect the field to the person. Obviously, there are no hard and fast rules here and design researchers will need to select the research design approach that is best suited to the research question. However, we hope that this chapter has challenged the field to examine exactly *who* sets the research question, *how* it is then conducted and disseminated and *why* change may be necessary. We believe that these questions for research design practice are important as we travel into this new decade and beyond.

Acknowledgements

We are grateful to Sage Publications for their permission to update the text and replicate the COINED model in this chapter (Figure 4.1) contained in the article by Caroline Swarbrick, Open Doors, EDUCATE, Katie Davis and John Keady (2019). The original article was published in the journal: *Dementia: The International Journal of Social Research and Practice* as online first in 2016 and then in hard copy in 2019. A full citation of this work is listed in the set of References to this chapter.

Additional reading (suggested)

Creswell, J. W and Creswell, J. D. (2017). *Research Design: Qualitative, Quantitative, and Mixed Methods Approaches*. Fifth Edition. London: Sage.
Kaplan, D. (2004). *The SAGE Handbook of Quantitative Methodology for the Social Sciences*. London: Sage.
Vogt, W. P. (2011). *SAGE Quantitative Research Methods*. London: Sage.

References

Aldridge, J. (2015). *Participatory Research: Working with Vulnerable Groups in Research and Practice*. Bristol University: Policy Press.
Bartlett, R. and O'Connor, D. (2010). *Broadening the Dementia Debate: Towards Social Citizenship*. Bristol: Policy Press.
Bethell. J., Commisso, E., Rostad, H. M., Puts, M., Babineau, J., Grinbergs-Saull, A., Wighton, M. B., Hammel, J., Doyle, E., Nadeau, S. and McGilton, K. S. (2018). Patient engagement in research related to dementia: a scoping review. *Dementia: The International Journal of Social Research and Practice*, 17 (8): 944–975.
Blair, T. and Minkler, M. (2009). Participatory action research with older adults: key principles in practice. *The Gerontologist*, 49 (5): 651–662.
Braun, V. and Clarke, V. (2019). Reflecting on reflexive thematic analysis. *Qualitative Research in Sport, Exercise and Health*, 11: 589–597.
Burton, A, Ogden, M. and Cooper, C. (2019). Planning and enabling meaningful patient and public involvement in dementia research. *Current Opinion in Psychiatry*, 32 (6): 557–562.
Chalfont, G. (2007). Wholistic design in dementia care. *Journal of Housing for the Elderly*, 21 (1/2): 153–177.
Charmaz, K. (2000). "Constructivist and objectivist grounded theory." In Denzin, N. K. and Lincoln, Y. S. (Eds.). *Handbook of Qualitative Research*, pp. 509–535. Second Edition. Thousand Oaks, CA: Sage.
Charmaz, K. (2006). *Constructing Grounded Theory: A Practical Guide through Qualitative Analysis*. London: Sage.
Clarke, C., Wilkinson, H., Watson, J., Wilcockson, J., Kinnaird, L. and Williamson, T. (2018). A seat around the table: participatory data analysis with people living with dementia. *Qualitative Health Research*, 28, 1421–1433.
Davies, S. (2009). "Foreword." In Staley, K. (report author) *Exploring Impact: Public Involvement in NHS, Public Health and Social Care Research*. Eastleigh: INVOLVE.
Davis, K. (2020). *Exploring the involvement of people living with dementia in research: A participatory study*. PhD thesis. Manchester, UK: The University of Manchester.
Department of Health. (2012). *Prime Minister's Challenge on Dementia. Delivering Major Improvements in Dementia Care and Research by 2015*. London: Department of Health.
Department of Health. (2015). *Prime Minister's Challenge on Dementia 2020*. London: Department of Health.
Department of Health. (2020). *UK Policy Framework for Health and Social Care Research*. London: Department of Health.
Dröes, R. M., Chattat, R., Diaz, A., Gove, D., Graff, M., Murphy, K., Verbeek, H., Vernooij-Dassen, M., Clare, L., Johannessen, A., Roes, M., Verhey, F. and

Charras, K. (2017). Social health and dementia: a European consensus on the operationalization of the concept and directions for research and practice. *Aging & Mental Health*, 21 (1): 4–17.

Foley, D. E. (2002). Critical ethnography: the reflexive turn. *International Journal of Qualitative Studies in Education*, 15 (4): 469–490.

Frank, L., Shubeck, E., Schicker, M., Webb, T., Maslow, K., Gitlin, L., Hummel, C. H., Kaplan, E. K., LeBlanc, B., Marquez, M. Nicholson, B., O'Brien, G., Phillips, L., Van Buren, B. and Epstein-Lubow, G. (2020). Contributions of persons living with dementia to scientific research meetings: best practices from the national research summit on care, services and supports for persons with dementia and their caregivers. *American Journal of Geriatric Psychiatry*, 28 (4): 421–430.

Freire, P. (1970). *Pedagogy of the Oppressed*. New York: Herder and Herder.

Glaser, B. G. (1978). *Theoretical Sensitivity*. Mill Valley, CA: Sociology Press.

Glaser, B. G. (1992). *Emergence vs Forcing: Basics of Grounded Theory Analysis*. Mill Valley, CA.: Sociology Press.

Glaser, B. G. and Strauss, A. L. (1967). *The Discovery of Grounded Theory: Strategies for Qualitative Research*. Chicago: Aldine.

Hall, B. L. and Kidd, R. J. (1978). *Adult Learning: A Design for Action*. Oxford: Pergamon.

Harris, P. and Sterin, G. (1999). Insider's perspective: defining and preserving the self in dementia. *Journal of Mental Health and Aging*, 5 (3): 241–256.

Heron, J. (1996). *Co-operative Inquiry: Research into the Human Condition*. London: Sage.

Higgins, P. (2013). Involving people with dementia in research. *Nursing Times*, 109 (28): 20–23.

Hassan Murad, M., Asi, N., Alsawas, M. and Alahdab, F. (2016). New evidence pyramid. *Evidence Based Medicine Online*, 10.1136/ebmed-2016-110401.

Hendriks, N., Huybrechts, L., Slegers, K., and Wilkinson, A. (2018). Valuing implicit decision-making in participatory design: a relational approach in design with people with dementia. *Design Studies*, 59: 58–76.

Hwang, A. S., Truong, K. N., and Mihailidis, A. (2012, May). "Using participatory design to determine the needs of informal caregivers for smart home user interfaces." In *2012 6th International Conference on Pervasive Computing Technologies for Healthcare (PervasiveHealth) and Workshops*, pp. 41–48. IEEE.

Iliffe, S., McGrath, T. and Mitchell, D. (2013). The impact of patient and public involvement in the work of the Dementias & Neurodegenerative Diseases Research Network (DeNDRoN): case studies. *Health Expectations*, 16 (4): 351–361.

INVOLVE. (2012). *Briefing Notes for Researchers: Public Involvement in NHS, Public Health and Social Care Research*. Eastleigh: INVOLVE.

Keady, J. and the Neighbourhoods and dementia study team. (2014). Neighbourhoods and dementia. *Journal of Dementia Care*, 22 (6): 16–17.

Kenning, G. (2018). Reciprocal design: inclusive design approaches for people with late stage dementia. *Design for Health*, 2 (1): 142–162.

Kitwood, T. (1997). *Dementia Reconsidered. The Person Comes First*. Buckingham: Open University Press.

Lindsay, S., Brittain, K., Jackson, D., Ladha, C., Ladha, K., and Olivier, P. (2012, May). "Empathy, participatory design and people with dementia." In *Proceedings of the SIGCHI Conference on Human Factors in Computing Systems*, New York. pp. 521–530.

Litherland, R., Burton, J., Cheeseman, M., Campbell, D., Hawkins, M., Hawkins, T., Oliver, K., Scott, D., Ward, J., Nelis, S. M., Quinn, C., Victor, C. and Clare, L. (2018). Reflections on PPI from the 'Action on Living Well: Asking You' advisory network of people with dementia and carers as part of the IDEAL study. *Dementia: The International Journal of Social Research and Practice*, 17 (8):1035–1044.

McKeown, J., Clarke., A., Ingleton, C. and Repper, J. (2010). Actively involving people with dementia in qualitative research. *Journal of Clinical Nursing*, 19: 1935–1943.

Maguire, P. (1987). *Doing Participatory Research: A Feminist Approach.* Available at: https://scholarworks.umass.edu/cie_participatoryresearchpractice/6/; accessed 24 July 2020.

May, T. and Perry, B. (2017). *Social Research and Reflexivity.* London: Sage.

Miah J, Dawes P, Edwards S, Leroi I, Starling B, Parsons S. (2019). Patient and public involvement in dementia research in the European Union: a scoping review. *BMC Geriatrics*, 19 (1): 220. doi.org: 10.1186/s12877-019-1217-9.

Morgan, D., Crossley, M., Stewart, N., Kirk, A., Forbes, D., D'Arcy, C. and Cammer, A. (2014). Evolution of a community-based participatory approach in a rural and remote dementia care research program. Progress in Community Health Partnerships. *Research, Education and Practice*, 8 (3): 337–345.

Muller, M. J., and Kuhn, S. (1993). Participatory design. *Communications of the ACM*, 36 (6), 24–28.

National Institute for Health and Care Excellence. (2018). *Dementia: Assessment, Management and Support for People Living with Dementia and their Carers.* NICE guideline. Published June 2018. Available at: www.nice.org.uk/guidance/ng97; accessed 24 July 2020.

Northway, R. (2008). "Participative Approaches to Research." In Watson, R., McKenna, H., Cowman, S. and Keady, J. (Eds.). *Nursing Research: Designs and Methods*, pp. 23–33. Edinburgh: Elsevier.

Reason, P. (1994). *Participation in Human Inquiry.* London: Sage Publications.

Reed, J. and Procter, S. (1995). *Practitioner Research in Health Care: The Inside Story.* London: Chapman and Hall.

Reilly, S. T., Harding, A. J. E., Morbey, H., Ahmed, F., Williamson, P. R., Swarbrick, C., Leroi, I., Davies, L., Reeves, D., Holland, F., Hann, M. and Keady, J. (2020).What is important to people with dementia living at home? A set of core outcome items for use in the evaluation of non-pharmacological community-based health and social care interventions. *Age and Ageing*, 1–8. doi: 10.1093/ageing/afaa.

Schuler, D. and Namioka, A. (1993). *Participatory Design: Principles and Practices*, Washington: Lawrence Erlbaum Associates.

The Scottish Dementia Working Group and The University of Edinburgh. (2013). Core principles for involving people with dementia in research: innovative practice. *Dementia: The International Journal of Social Research and Practice*, 13 (5): 680–685.

Simonsen, J., and Robertson, T. (Eds.). 2012. *Routledge International Handbook of Participatory Design.* Routledge.

Span, M., Hettinga, M., Groen-van de Ven, L., Jukema, J., Janssen, R., Vernooij-Dassen, M., Eefsting, J. and Smits, C. (2018). Involving people with dementia in developing an interactive web tool for shared decision-making: experiences with a participatory design approach. *Disability and Rehabilitation*, 40 (12): 1410–1420.

Stoecker, R. (1999). Are academics irrelevant? Roles for scholars in participatory research. *American Behavioral Scientist*, 42 (5): 840–854.

Strauss, A. and Corbin, J. (1990). *Basics of Qualitative Research: Grounded Theory Procedures and Techniques*. London: Sage.

Swaffer, K. (2016). Co-production and engagement of people with dementia: the issue of ethics and creative or intellectual copyright. *Dementia: The International Journal of Social Research and Practice*, 15 (6): 1319–1325.

Swarbrick, C. M., Open Doors, EDUCATE, Davis, K. and Keady, J. (2019). Visioning change: co-producing a model of involvement and engagement in research. *Dementia: The International Journal of Social Research and Practice* (Innovative Practice), 18 (7–8): 3165–3172.

Swarbrick, C. M., Open Doors Dementia Service, Khetani, B., Riley, C. and Keady, J. (2020). Reflections on the ethics of co-research alongside people living with dementia. *SAGE Research Methods Cases: Medicine and Health*, 2020: online peer reviewed publication available at: doi: https://dx.doi.org/10.4135/9781529709209.

Tanner, D. (2012). Co-research with older people with dementia: experience and reflections. *Journal of Mental Health*, 21 (3): 296–306.

Thorne, S. (2008). *Interpretive Description*. Walnut Creek, CA: Left Coast Press.

Waite, J., Poland, F. and Charlesworth, G. (2019). Facilitators and barriers to co-research by people with dementia and academic researchers: findings from a qualitative study. *Health Expectations*, 22 (4): 761–771.

Watson, R. and Keady, J. (2008). "The Language of Research." In Watson, R., McKenna, H., Cowman, S. and Keady, J. (Eds.). *Nursing Research: Designs and Methods*, pp. 3–12. Edinburgh: Elsevier.

Webb, J., Williams, V., Gall, M. and Dowling, S. (2020). Misfitting the research process: shaping qualitative research "in the field" to fit people living with dementia. *International Journal of Qualitative Methods*, 19: 1–11

Williams, S. and Keady, J. (2021). "Participatory case study work: What it is, how it functions and our adaptations to the approach." In Williams, S. and Keady, J. (Eds.). *Participatory Case Study Research: Approaches, Authenticity and Application in Ageing Studies*, pp. 12–29. Routledge: London.

Windle, G., Newman, A., Burholt, V., Woods, B., O'Brien, D., Baber, M., Hounsome, B., Parkinson, C. and Tischler, V. (2016). Dementia and Imagination: a mixed-methods protocol for arts and science research. *BMJ Open*, 6 (11): e011634. doi: 10.1136/bmjopen-2016–011634.

Woods, R. T., Orrell, M., Bruce, E., Edwards, R. T., Hoare, Z., Hounsome, B., Keady, J., Moniz-Cook, E., Orgeta, V., Rees, J. and Russell, I. T. (2016). REMCARE: pragmatic multi-centre randomised trial of reminiscence groups for people with dementia and their family carers: effectiveness and economic analysis. *PLoS ONE*, 11 (4): e0152843. doi: 10.1371/journal.pone.0152843.

Wright, D., Foster, C., Amir, Z., Elliott, J. and Wilson, R. (2010). Critical appraisal guidelines for assessing the quality and impact of user involvement in research. *Health Expectations*, 13: 359–368.

5 Things

Design interventions against dementia

Introduction

Drawing from the design research literature four key research themes have been identified, where design research effort has focused. These include:

- Reminiscence and personhood
- Social interaction and living in the moment
- Independent and assisted living
- Cognitive and physical stimulation

Several other relevant design research projects not fitting or focusing on any of the aforementioned themes have been included under a miscellaneous theme.

Given the subject, the literature review focused on design research related journals and conferences, which were systematically searched from January 2010 to December 2019. Examples of journals include: *The International Journal of Design, The Design Journal, Journal of Design Research, Design Issues, Design Studies, Design for Health, International Journal of Arts and Technology, CoDesign, Dementia* and examples of conference proceedings searched include: the European Academy Design, Design4Health, Design Research Society, the Design of Interactive Systems and Computer Human Interaction.

After the literary search was completed and the papers selected, the data analysis commenced based on the thematic analysis methodology by Braun and Clarke (2006). Thematic coding was done by looking at each paragraph and coding data by writing notes through the use of either sticky notes or electronic notes within the electronic version of the paper. After the data coding and collation, overarching themes started to emerge. For inclusion, a theme should have been discussed in length by at least three or more articles (See Table 5.1). In the initial theme search several more sub-themes were identified, however the main themes were integrated into larger themes to allow for clarity and consistency. The themes are discussed in more detail in the following sections.

Table 5.1 Non-pharmacological dementia interventions developed through design research

No.	Paper	Intervention	Research method(s)	Themes				
				Reminiscence and personhood	Social interaction and living in the moment	Independent and assisted living	Cognitive and physical stimulation	Miscellaneous
1	Anderiessen, H., Scherder, E., Goossens, R., Visch, V. and Eggermont, L. 2015. Play experiences for people with Alzheimer's disease. *International Journal of Design*, 9 (2): 155–165.	Game design heuristics						x
2	Branco, R. M., Quental, J. and Ribeiro, Ó. 2017. Personalised participation: an approach to involve people with dementia and their families in a participatory design project. *CoDesign*, 13 (2): 127–143.	A range of visual prototypes, including personalised card game, a personalised board game	Participatory design		x			
3	Brankaert, R. G. A. and de Jong, H. J. 2015. "A Point in the Right Direction: A Simple Navigation Device for People with Dementia." In *Third European Conference on Design4health*, 13–16 July 2015, Sheffield, UK.	A navigation system prototype with auditory feedback	Iterative prototyping and field study with eight participants			x		

(continued)

#	Reference	Description	Design approach			
4	Casiddu, N. and Porfirione, C. 2017. Design for Dysphagia: a new hardware-and-software mobile system to monitor patients' swallowing. *The Design Journal*, 20 (sup1): S2078-S2089.	A new hardware/ software mobile system to monitor patients' swallowing	User-centred design			x
5	Darby, A. G. and Tsekleves, E. 2018. "Mentian: Developing Design Fiction for Dementia Policy." In *Proceedings of the Design Research Society Conference 2018: Design Research Society Conference Proceedings 2018*, pp. 2407–2421, 6. Limerick: Design Research Society.	A design fiction on dementia policy	Participatory design and speculative design			x
6	Favilla, S. and Pedell, S. 2013. "Touch Screen Ensemble Music: Collaborative Interaction for Older People with Dementia." In *Proceedings of the 25th Australian Computer-Human Interaction Conference: Augmentation, Application, Innovation, Collaboration*, pp. 481–484.	New iPad controllers and interactive music software aimed at engaging people with dementia	Participatory design	x	X	

Table 5.1 Cont.

No.	Paper	Intervention	Research method(s)	Themes				
				Reminiscence and personhood	Social interaction and living in the moment	Independent and assisted living	Cognitive and physical stimulation	Miscellaneous
7	Garde, J. A., Van Der Voort, M. C. and Niedderer, K. 2018. "Design Probes for People with Dementia." In *Proceedings of the Design Research Society Conference 2018: Design Research Society Conference Proceedings 2018*, pp. 2607–2621, 6. Limerick: Design Research Society.		Design probes	X	X	x		
8	Gowans, G., Dye, R., Alm, N., Vaughan, P., Astell, A. and Ellis, M. 2007. Designing the interface between dementia patients, caregivers and computer-based intervention. *The Design Journal*, 10 (1): 12–23.	Computer-based assistive tools for people with dementia to support progressive, non-pharmacological intervention and promote improved quality of life in dementia care environments	Iterative prototyping, usability testing	X	x			

(continued)

9	Hanson, E., Magnusson, L., Arvidsson, H., Claesson, A., Keady, J. and Nolan, M. 2007. Working together with persons with early stage dementia and their family members to design a user-friendly technology-based support service. *Dementia*, 6 (3): 411–434.	A technology-based information, education and support service	Action participatory research	x
10	Hattink, B. J. J., Meiland, F. J. M., Overmars-Marx, T., de Boer, M., Ebben, P. W. G., van Blanken, M., Verhaeghe, S., Stalpers-Croeze, I., Jedlitschka, A., Flick, S. E., v/d Leeuw, J., Karkowski, I. and Droes, R. M 2016. The electronic, personalizable Rosetta system for dementia care: exploring the user-friendliness, usefulness and impact. *Disability and Rehabilitation: Assistive Technology*, 11 (1): 61–71.	Integrated assistive technology (AT) systems which can support people with dementia and carers throughout the course of dementia	Controlled trial with pre-and post-test, questionnaires, semi-structured interviews	x

Table 5.1 Cont.

No.	Paper	Intervention	Research method(s)	Themes				
				Reminiscence and personhood	Social interaction and living in the moment	Independent and assisted living	Cognitive and physical stimulation	Miscellaneous
11	Iltanen-Tähkävuori, S., Wikberg, M. and Topo, P. 2012. Design and dementia: A case of garments designed to prevent undressing. *Dementia*, 11 (1): 49–59.	Patient overall is to prevent undressing in socially inappropriate situations and/or to stop the user from removing incontinence pads	Material and design audit, interviews with designers of medical textiles, interviews			x		
12	Jakob, A. and Collier, L. 2017. Sensory enrichment for people living with dementia: increasing the benefits of multisensory environments in dementia care through design. *Design for Health*, 1 (1): 115–133.	Evaluation of the impact of design on providing multisensory experience for people with dementia living in care homes, particularly the quality of multisensory environments (MSEs)	Ethnographic methods (semi-structured, in-depth, face-to-face interviews with care home staff, observation)		x		X	

No.	Reference	Intervention	Method			
13	Kenning, G. 2018. Reciprocal design: inclusive design approaches for people with late stage dementia. *Design for Health*, 2 (1): 1–21.	A range of multisensory prototypes aimed at providing opportunities for social interaction and engagement	Action research, participatory design	x	x	X
14	Kenning, G. and Treadaway, C. 2018. Designing for dementia: iterative grief and transitional objects. *Design Issues*, 34 (1): 42–53.	Sensory textiles for people with advanced dementia	Participatory design, interview, observation, and case studies	x	X	X
15	King, A. P. Y. and Siu, K. W. M. 2017. Participant observation in cognitive gameplay as a rehabilitation tool for living alone elderly with dementia in Hong Kong: a pilot study. *The Design Journal*, 20 (sup1): S2426–S2438.		Participatory action research, semi-structured interviews	x	x	
16	Lazar, A., Thompson, H. and Demiris, G. 2014. A systematic review of the use of technology for reminiscence therapy. *Health Education & Behavior*, 41 (1_suppl): 51S–61S.	Systematically examines the scientific literature on the use of ICT for facilitating Reminiscence Therapy	Systematic literature review. A total of 386 articles were retrieved, 44 of which met the inclusion and exclusion criteria	x		

(continued)

Table 5.1 Cont.

No.	Paper	Intervention	Research method(s)	Themes				
				Reminiscence and personhood	*Social interaction and living in the moment*	*Independent and assisted living*	*Cognitive and physical stimulation*	*Miscellaneous*
17	Mihailidis, A., Blunsden, S., Boger, J., Richards, B., Zutis, K., Young, L. and Hoey, J. 2010. Towards the development of a technology for art therapy and dementia: Definition of needs and design constraints. *The Arts in Psychotherapy,* 37 (4): 293–300.	Computer-based tool for use in arts therapy with older adults who have dementia	Survey and prototyping			x		
18	Morrissey, K., Wood, G., Green, D., Pantidi, N. and McCarthy, J. 2016, June. "'I'm a Rambler, I'm a Gambler, I'm a Long Way from Home' The Place of Props, Music, and Design in Dementia Care." In *Proceedings of the 2016 ACM Conference on Designing Interactive Systems,* pp. 1008–1020.	Multisensory music based prototype encouraging movement	Design ethnography (observations), participatory workshops		x			

(continued)

	Reference	Description	Methods			
19	Müller-Rakow, A. and Flechtner, R. 2017. Designing interactive music systems with and for people with dementia. *The Design Journal*, 20 (sup1): S2207–S2214.	Interactive and networked music system for people with dementia – music therapy	Participatory design, personas, use cases, prototyping	x	X	
20	Murko, P. and Kunze, C. 2015, July. "Tangible Memories: Exploring the Use of Tangible Interfaces for Occupational Therapy in Dementia Care." In *Proceedings of the 3rd European Conference on Design4Health* (Vol. 13, p. 16).	Surface computing and tangible interfaces for people living with dementia	Prototyping, evaluation and usability testing	X	x	
21	Oven, P. Č. and Predan, B. 2015. "A Set of Social Games for Senior Citizens with Dementia/D9." In *Proceedings of the 3rd European Conference on Design4Health* (Vol. 13).	3D physical games prototypes	Prototyping	X	X	x
22	Pedro, M., Costa, A and Lopes, L 2015. "Dementia – Stimulation of Memories." In *Third European Conference on Design4health*, 13–16 July 2015, Sheffield, UK.	Product developed with the purpose of stimulating and exercising the memory of people living with dementia	Participatory design, ethnographic design	X	x	

Table 5.1 Cont.

No.	Paper	Intervention	Research method(s)	Themes				
				Reminiscence and personhood	Social interaction and living in the moment	Independent and assisted living	Cognitive and physical stimulation	Miscellaneous
23	Rodgers, P. A. 2018. Co-designing with people living with dementia. *CoDesign*, 14 (3): 188–202.	Development of tartan by people living with dementia	Co-design and prototyping	x				X
24	Smeenk, W., Sturm, J. and Eggen, B. 2017. Empathic handover: how would you feel? Handing over dementia experiences and feelings in empathic co-design. *CoDesign*, 14 (4): 1–16.	Dementia simulator	Co-design					X
25	Subramaniam, P. and Woods, B. 2010. Towards the therapeutic use of information and communication technology in reminiscence work for people with dementia: a systematic review. *International Journal of Computers in Healthcare*, 1 (2): 106–125.		Paper reviews on reminiscence therapy (11 studies included)	x				

(*continued*)

#	Reference	Design outcome	Methods		
26	Tobiasson, H., Sundblad, Y., Walldius, A. and Hedman, A. 2015. Designing for active life: moving and being moved together with dementia patients. *International Journal of Design*, 9 (3): 47–62.	Exergames (Nintendo Wii).	Participatory design, interviews, citations, field notes, photographs and videos	x	X
27	Treadaway, C., Prytherch, D., Kenning, G. and Fennell, J. 2016. In the moment: designing for late stage dementia. In *Proceedings of DRS2016: Design+ Research+ Society-Future-Focused Thinking* (Vol. 8). Design Research Society.	Playful artefacts that will contribute to non-pharmacological personalised approaches to caring for people living with late-stage dementia in residential care	Participatory design	x	X
28	Van der Linden, V., Van Steenwinkel, I., Dong, H. and Heylighen, A. 2016, June. "Designing 'Little Worlds' in Walnut Park: How Architects Adopted an Ethnographic Case Study on Living with Dementia." In *Proceedings of DRS2016: Design Research Society-Future-Focused Thinking* (Vol. 8, pp. 3199–3212). Design Research Society.	Ethnographic case study, interviews	x	X	

Table 5.1 Cont.

No.	Paper	Intervention	Research method(s)	Themes					
				Reminiscence and personhood	Social interaction and living in the moment	Independent and assisted living	Cognitive and physical stimulation	Miscellaneous
29	van Hoof, J., Blom, M. M., Post, H. N. and Bastein, W. L. 2013. Designing a 'Think-Along Dwelling' for people with dementia: a co-creation project between health care and the building services sector. *Journal of Housing for the Elderly*, 27 (3): 299–332.	Design incorporating modifications in terms of architecture, interior design, the indoor environment and technological solutions	This study reports the design process of a demonstration home for people with dementia through performing a literature review and focus group sessions			X		

Note: "X" denotes that this is the main theme in the paper. "x" denotes that this is a secondary theme in the paper.

Reminiscence and personhood

Despite pharmacological interventions having received most research attention and funding, there is increasing evidence that psychological interventions may be equally effective, with 'reminiscence therapy' being widely used in practice and now receiving attention from researchers (Subramaniam and Woods, 2010) although the outcomes from a large multi-centre reminiscence trial remain mixed (Woods et al., 2016). This may be because present outcome measures do not fully capture embodied and in-the-moment experiences that are centred around creativity (group and individual) and fun. Such outcome development would add much to the literature.

Typically, under the umbrella term of reminiscence therapy, there is a wide variety of therapeutic activities which may include the discussion of past activities, personally significant people, events and experiences. This is usually done with the aid of tangible prompts such as photographs, household and other familiar items from the past, music and archive sound recordings (Lazar et al., 2014). The introduction of digital technologies in reminiscence work has enabled the digitisation of such prompts, especially photographs, music and videos. Reminiscence therapy can focus on a single individual, becoming more personalised or it can focus on a group becoming a more social and shared activity in a group setting.

A systematic literature review by Subramaniam and Woods (2010) has revealed a great variety of reminiscence therapy interventions/prompts being used, including individual picture gramophone; biography theatre; therapeutic/restorative biographies; personalised reminiscence video; personalised multimedia biographies; multimedia biography; personal TV photograph album; digital life histories; and interactive life story multimedia. It has shown that reminiscence activities are mainly used to maintain the identity of the person living with dementia, for encouraging communication with other people living with dementia and care staff. An additional advantage of reminiscence therapy is that it can be used with people with varying levels of cognition, including those who have lost ability to verbalize (Lazar et al., 2014).

Challenges remain however as personalised materials require a significant resource commitment in terms of developing the biography with the person living with dementia, with additional input from the family. Furthermore, individualised reminiscence therapy sessions are demanding in terms of staff or carer resources. Digitising reminiscence prompts can potentially help in replacing or augmenting current aspects of reminiscence work (i.e. through life story books, multisensory memory triggers) and provide a new dimension of private reminiscence work that can be facilitated by these systems reducing staff resources. However, this is currently under researched.

In relation to this, the systematic literature review by Lazar et al. (2014) has examined the use of digital technologies for facilitating reminiscence therapy. A quarter of the papers they reviewed reported the use of a technological component in a reminiscence kit, some using kits available commercially, while others used reminiscence kits developed by the researchers.

Lazar et al. (2014) also found that reminiscence research using digital technologies provides five key benefits:

1. Accommodating for deficits: using technology to ease participation: mitigate motor and sensory impairments, compensate for memory deficits.
2. Sensory awareness and musical responsiveness. Media (photos, audio, video) were used as triggers to prompt a positive response in the form of interactions or improved mood.
3. Emotional memory. Projects that focused on this ability mainly appealed to something personally relevant to the individual.
4. Easing the burden of therapy delivery. Technology can bridge geographic distance and address transportation barriers.
5. Evaluating progress and use. Technology can be used to track and monitor progress and system use.

As such, in recent years there has been interest in the design research community to explore further the design of interventions and experiences for reminiscence therapy. For example, Gowans et al. (2007) have designed and developed a computer-driven reminiscence intervention aimed at promoting improved quality of life in dementia care environments. Using iterative prototyping and usability testing, 40 people living with dementia and 30 caregivers were recruited to participate in, and evaluate, the prototypes. Following an analysis of their testing sessions, they found that their intervention managed to prompt memories from a number of individuals, which none of the caregivers had heard before. It helped to involve people who would not normally react poorly to traditional reminiscence intervention. As a result of their work they have offered some design recommendations for the design of reminiscence interventions (see Gowans et al. 2007).

In another design research related project, Murko and Kunze (2015) have explored the application of surface computing and tangible interfaces for people living with dementia. Following a literature review, qualitative interviews were conducted with five experts in the field of dementia in order to collect experiences about needs of people living with dementia and to help develop ideas for possible interventions. This led to the creation of three personas and validated with the experts, in order to help develop a better understanding of the user group. Three application prototypes were designed, implemented and tested during a two-week trial period with the use of a surface computer in an elderly care facility in order to examine the usability and the impact on people living with dementia. A total of 14 participants at different stages of dementia were included in the evaluation. The user testing demonstrated that the interventions led to enjoyable conversations between caregivers and residents and encouraged stumbling onto old memories. The results show considerable effects in terms of increasing interaction of the participants compared to conventional touch-screen applications.

Similarly, Pedro et al. (2015) developed a memory stimulation intervention aimed at enhancing the interaction between people living with dementia, their caregivers and their families. Through observation and participatory activities with people living with dementia they identified those activities that served like stimulation with the purpose of reducing memory loss. Through iterative prototyping and testing they explored different concepts and approaches, helping to adjust the relation between the memory object and user needs. This led to the development of the 'PlayMemo', a tangible memory game-type intervention. The paper claimed that its testing showed that it enabled memory stimulation and promoted healthy interaction, while strengthening users' reasoning skills and deduction capabilities. They also reported that caregivers, who helped to conduct the tests, noticed right from the beginning, the impact of the intervention to the patients, stating that it was a stimulating activity not only for people living with dementia but for others as well (Pedro et al., 2015).

Social interaction and living in the moment

Interest in supporting social interaction and living in the moment through design-based interventions and research has been shown by the design research community as well. Some projects have explored this area through the development of interventions, engaging different senses through physical and/or physical-digital objects (Oven and Predan, 2015; Kenning and Treadaway, 2018), with some developing new design research methodologies to engage people living with dementia in research, whilst others have focused on the development of interventions engaging and stimulation social interaction through music (Favilla and Pedell, 2013; Morrissey et al., 2016; Müller-Rakow and Flechtner, 2017).

More precisely, Oven and Predan (2015) have explored the design of physical game-based intervention that creates a set of social activities for stimulating social interaction between people living with dementia and their caregivers (professional or family). They have employed a combination of desk-based (literature review) and qualitative methods (observation, focus groups with stakeholders) to iteratively design and develop a 3D working prototype of a game based on identified areas of interest/conversation for people living with dementia (i.e. food, objects, animals, emotions, the seasons and specific events). These were designed in such a way in order to encourage new game variations created by inventive therapists and family members as well as personalized variations that will suit different individuals from different cultures. The 3D objects (cubes) were developed to be hollow and from different material that stimulate the sense of smell and touch. Field-testing of the different versions and difficulty levels of the games, suggested that a well-designed activity set could be a positive tool and provide much-needed assistance to family members and professional caregivers (Oven and Predan, 2015).

Within, the theme of stimulation the senses and living in the moment, Kenning and Treadaway (2018) have conducted research on the development of sensory textiles for people living with advanced dementia. This was achieved through the use of interpretative qualitative methodologies including semi-structured interviews (with key care staff, the care facility manager and occupational therapists), observation, case studies from different care facilities, as well as seven participatory events were held over a period of one year. Two blanket objects were designed to help support people living with dementia as they approached the end of life and their families. The materials chosen in the construction of the sensory textile object fulfilled the need of people in the later stages of dementia with basic comfort and soothing, by offering fabrics, such as chenille, that are warm and pleasant to touch. Their findings from testing the two blanket interventions, showed that the objects promoted engagement and interaction between the person living with dementia and the object, as well as between the person living with dementia and their family members and carers. The objects became a point of focus during a time of transition and transformation and when death occurred, they acted as a memorial to the latter stages of life of the person with dementia. The personalisation of the objects encouraged participants in the study to focus fully on their intimate and personal time together. Focusing on personalisation supported the retention of a persons' identity, even when they could no longer remember or communicate their past. This study demonstrated how sensory objects can enable people in the latter stages of life to connect socially, engage meaningfully with objects, and experience pleasure and the importance of maintaining a sense of personhood throughout their life time (Kenning and Treadaway, 2018).

Moving onto the subject of music therapy, Müller-Rakow and Flechtner (2017) explored the development of an interactive and networked music system for people living with dementia. Employing, participatory design, scenarios, and personas, paper prototypes (cf. Snyder, 2003) and mock-ups they developed their music therapy intervention. Based on their observations during the workshops and interviews they conceptualised a framework for interfaces that aim at compensating the loss of technical know-how and the ability to interact with music systems. Their research from the observation sessions and iterative prototyping workshops revealed that most participants were unable to initiate listening sessions or to remember and organise music therapy sessions. Furthermore, their secondary research showed that there is a divergence between potential therapeutic intervention and psychological well-being through music on the one hand, and a significant absence of music in the everyday lives of people living with dementia on the other hand. This was despite a profound desire for musical experiences. Their testing showed some usability related issues and levels of playfulness based on interactive prototypes that differ in complexity and form. They used the lessons they learnt to share proposals for designing music-based interventions with and for people living with dementia (Müller-Rakow and Flechtner, 2017).

Favilla and Pedell (2013) also explored the topic of music therapy through the development of new iPad controllers and interactive music software aimed at engaging people living with dementia. They ran several participatory workshops with group of 12–14 elderly people living with dementia and their carers. During the sessions the group was given 12 iPads to explore the iteratively developed intervention. Interactions and performances were recorded for study comparisons. Their findings suggest that people living with dementia are able to successfully perform and engage in collaborative music performance activities with little or no scaffolded instruction. They also demonstrated that careful attention to sound, collaborative interaction and touchscreen control are essential for success (Favilla and Pedell, 2013).

In their case study Morrissey et al. (2016) employed music to stimulate physical movement and social interaction. Employing design ethnography (observations) and participatory workshops, they began to carry out music workshops alongside ongoing observation of daily life in the elderly care facility. Field notes along with conversational data was also collected and then organised and analysed using Grounded Theory techniques. This led to the design of an interactive intervention (SwaytheBand) aimed at encourage participants to sway or otherwise move to music being played by a computer system by illustrating a song's tempo using a series of sequenced coloured light flashes to correspond to changes in music beat. During the song people living with dementia (band members) held a PlayStation Move controller, whose LED light at its top changed colour in time to the beat of the music, inviting arm movement. Their findings show how participation in music sessions for people living with dementia can take many forms (touch, moving, inhabiting roles, interacting with materials and more subtle forms of participation). Further, this work shows how simple and digital props can engage participants living with dementia to participate in several ways in music sessions but notably create participation that is meaningful to them and provide researchers with ways to leverage this meaningfulness in design.

Independent and assisted living

This theme forms one of the most popular areas for design research with several projects looking into fostering independence and assisted living for people living with dementia. Some research focuses on how this can be better enabled through ensuring wider participation of people living with dementia in the design process (Hanson et al., 2007; Branco et al., 2017; Garde et al., 2018); interior design and architecture modification to provide more independence for people living with dementia (van Hoof et al., 2013; Van der Linden et al., 2016); digital tools for art therapy (Michailidis et al., 2010); developing assistive technology systems to support people living with dementia and carers throughout the course of dementia (Hattink, et al., 2016); and a navigation device for people living with dementia (Brankaert and de Jong, 2015).

Designing with people has encouraged design researchers to think carefully about how to make participation happen in a respectful, ethical and empathic way but also how materials can be redesigned and, considering the uniqueness of each family, how the process can be pleasurable and open enough for participants to personalise their participation. Hanson et al. (2007) have employed participatory action research to actively involve people living with early stage dementia throughout the entire research and development process of designing a user-friendly technology-based information, education and support service. Their preliminary findings revealed that older people living with early-stage dementia can learn and benefit from user-friendly technology, especially when used together with others in a similar situation. Their results also reinforce the importance of developing more creative support services that challenge traditional stereotypes and serve to empower frail older people and their carers.

Branco et al. (2017) have developed a personalised approach to participatory design, where several aspects of the project, such as brief, process and artefacts, are left open to be redefined by the participants, in accordance with their individual needs, preferences and availabilities. In this approach, people living with dementia are not merely an object of study. Instead, they are invited to be at the centre of the project together with their families, bringing their voices and their stories. Garde et al. (2018) employed a different means of encouraging more active participation by developing design probes. These were designed to provide insight into the perspectives and life of people living with dementia to enable a more empathic design approach and to identify needs, opportunities and ideas for mindful design interventions. These were intended to provide enjoyment in completing these, personal reflection, the generation of something that they and their family can keep as a memory and, more active participation in the design process. Analysis of their probes and follow-up interviews revealed some challenges in the design of probes for people living with dementia, such as developing adequate responses to the questions/tasks set. However, they also revealed that design probes can offer an aspect of self-empowerment, as they can be done in a self-directed manner, at the time the person living with dementia wants to or feels best, by self-deciding what the focus of the answer should be, and even by deciding not to do it. This was found to be easier for people living with dementia than being confronted with an interview situation that requires immediate focus and answers (Garde et al., 2018). Similarly, the personalised approach to participatory design that Braco et al. (2017) developed emerged from a need to involve people with dementia and their families in a participatory design project. This was also undertaken holding values that related to respectfulness, empathy and conviviality.

Designing the built environment to better accommodate the needs of people living with dementia has gained traction in the interior design/urban design research community with the focus been on the interior design of the home encouraging ageing at home (van Hoof et al., 2013) and of more responsive residential care facilities (Van der Linden et al., 2016). More precisely, van Hoof et al. (2013) study reports the design process of a demonstration home for people living with dementia aiming to design a home for people living with dementia that supports ageing-in-place that could be used as a demonstration dwelling for training and education. Their design conducted through performing a literature review and focus group sessions, incorporates modifications in terms of architecture, interior design, the indoor environment, and technological solutions. Their literature review revealed that most design guidelines were frequently based on small-scale studies, and, therefore, more systematic field research should be performed to provide further evidence for the efficacy of solutions. The design process of the dementia demonstration dwelling on one had has shown that it is possible to integrate evidence-based architectural and technological solutions, which support both individuals living with dementia and their carers in daily life situations. On the other hand, it has served as an educational and training setting for professionals from the fields of nursing, construction and building services engineering.

In contrast, Van der Linden et al. (2016) have explored the process of designing a residential care facility by architects and how this can be further supported involving people living with dementia in the process. They ran an ethnographic case study and conducted interviews with the architects. Their results indicate that an ethnographic case study can offer architects insight into the daily life of a person living with dementia that are transferable to a new design situation. Moreover, it can facilitate architects' concept development. The architects' conceptual drawing illustrates the transformative character of the knowledge embedded in the case study, from the person living with dementia's involvement in the research to the architects' active adoption. The study contributes to untangling important aspects in informing architects about future users and raises questions regarding researchers' and designers' roles in transferring knowledge.

Moving on to specific design interventions that promote independent and assisted living one encounters, Mihailidis et al. (2010) conducted work on the identification of desirable features and functionalities of a computer-based tool for use in arts therapy with older adults living with dementia. Using a multi-national survey with artists, therapists and people living with dementia and ethnographic analysis of the data, three prototype devices were developed. From the survey it was identified that this new technology should focus on painting and drawing activities, as these were the creative activities that survey respondents felt older adults living with dementia would enjoy the most.

Therapist interactions should also involve the option of 'co-creation' of art between the user and therapist using the device. Analysis of the prototype sessions evaluation showed such intervention can provide more frequent access to therapeutic entertainment in their own free time, giving people living with dementia a greater feeling of independence and satisfaction. They can also enable therapists to reach more clients and to facilitate therapeutic interventions more efficiently.

Research by Hattink et al. (2016) integrated previously developed assistive technology (AT) systems into one modular, multifunctional system, to support people living with dementia and carers throughout the course of dementia. In an explorative evaluation study, the integrated system, called Rosetta, was tested on usefulness, user-friendliness and impact, in people living with dementia, their informal carers and professional carers involved. The system was installed in participants' homes in three countries (the Netherlands, Germany and Belgium) and evaluated by employing pre- and post-test measures along with participants completing questionnaires for impact measurement and participating in semi-structured interviews regarding the system's usefulness and user-friendliness. Both people living with dementia and their informal carers considered a system like Rosetta useful to help maintain independence by reminding people living with dementia of appointments, which informal carers can remotely set.

Brankaert and de Jong (2015) designed a simple navigation device for people living with dementia. Following an iterative design process several prototypes were created and evaluated with experts and users. After this process, a field study was performed with eight participants using a working prototype. The results from the test showed that most participants managed to fulfil the tasks, however, there were still moments of confusion. Furthermore, the chosen metaphor, a compass, seemed viable for navigation: participants were capable and willing to follow the device. A number of design recommendations were also developed.

Cognitive and physical stimulation

Designers have also engaged with research on the development of cognitive and physical stimulation interventions. These include research on: stimulating physical movement through video games (Tobiasson et al., 2015); cognitive stimulation through more traditional tangible games (King and Siu, 2017); multisensory environments in care homes (Jakob and Collier, 2017); and research on the design of playful artefacts for cognitive and physical stimulation for people living with late-stage dementia in residential care (Treadaway et al., 2016). This latter work will be returned to in Part 2 of the book and the case study on the LAUGH project.

More precisely, Tobiasson et al. (2015) conducted in Sweden a number of case studies with dementia care facilities using Nintendo Wii Sports as an exergaming platform, in order to stimulate movement. They employed a participatory design approach through workshops, field notes, photographs, videos and interviews with participants such as managers, nurses, rehabilitation assistants and physiotherapists. They then carried out the thematic analysis based on empirical data that was generated through different methods. Their findings showed that the use of exergames in care settings managed to bridge the gap between 'being cared for' and being 'active in life'. It managed to create the feelings of 'being in control' and 'handling the situation' for older people who often have to cope with losing their abilities. Furthermore, their results indicated that the notions of games/competition, social interaction, physical activity and challenges are valuable ingredients when designing for the well-being of older people who suffer from moderate to severe dementia.

In a related project, King and Siu (2017) explored the use of cognitive gameplay as a rehabilitation tool for living older people alone with dementia in Hong Kong. Using design ethnography several older people living alone with dementia were observed playing four existing gameplays in a natural setting, followed by semi-structured interviews. Following a participatory design approach several physiotherapists, social workers, centre staffs, carers in a typical dementia care centre and designer took part in design process of revamping existing game sets through iteration. Their research showed that many of the game sets used in a traditional elderly day-care dementia centre in Hong Kong did not satisfy the foundation meaning of cognitive training, due to lack of universal design consideration. Their research findings also include suggestion on how to improve participation in gameplay among elderly persons living with dementia by improving the designs of current play tools.

Following on from the context of dementia care homes, Jakob and Collier (2017) investigated the impact of design on providing multisensory experience for people living with dementia in these, through multisensory environments (MSEs). Within the South UK, 16 care homes participated in their study. Data were collected using ethnographic methods including semi-structured, in-depth, face-to-face interviews with care home staff, observations from the perspective of the user, and recording examples of successful practice. Their findings revealed two key issues. Firstly, that the set-up and design of existing MSEs in care environments is, in most cases, not suitable for older people. Secondly, that there is a lack of knowledge and information for care practitioners in facilitating sensory activities and environments. Based on these findings, design criteria improving usability and accessibility for people living with dementia were established and user-centred design recommendations developed.

Moreover, personalised approaches to caring for people living with late-stage dementia through the development of playful artefacts has been explored in residential care by Treadaway et al. (2016). Following an inclusive participatory methodology, 25 key experts, such as health professionals, technologists, materials scientists and carers of people living with dementia, informed the development of design concepts via a series of participatory workshops. Also visits and interviews in the care homes, a series of Live Lab evaluations and team reflections were used to gather data. Audio and video recording, collaborative creative worksheets capturing ideas and commentary, participant feedback sheets, still photography and research journals were used as research tools in the process. Seven playful objects were developed with observations acquired during the Live Lab evaluations (Treadaway et al., 2019). The initial stages of the research have identified the significance of playfulness, sensory stimulation, hand use and emotional memory. Following their findings, Treadaway et al. (2016) posit that designs should aim to promote 'in the moment' living in order to support subjective well-being of people living with late-stage dementia.

Miscellaneous

A plethora of design research projects that do not focus in any of the four themes presented below are also found in the literature. Some of these deal with the development of specific solutions for people living with dementia, such as garments for people living with dementia in care homes (Iltanen-Tähkävuori et al., 2012), helping people with swallowing food issues (Casiddu and Porfirione, 2017); others focus on exploring the play experiences persons in different stages of dementia enjoy and value (Anderiesen et al., 2015); whilst others focused on the exploration of design research methods within the context of dementia, such as co-design (Smeenk et al., 2017; Rodgers, 2018), reciprocal design (Kenning, 2018) and speculative design (Darby and Tsekleves, 2018).

Looking at the former, Iltanen-Tähkävuori et al. (2012) explored the design of a patient overall that will prevent people living with dementia to undress in socially inappropriate situations and/or to stop them from removing an incontinence pad. They conducted material and design audit, interviews with designers of medical textiles and with people with experience of wearing medical textiles, and their regular visitors in the care institutions. Their research revealed that the original design of the patient overalls was based on the needs expressed by carers, not by the people wearing them. Although the use of a patient overall benefits family carers and care staff by making it possible to control the wearer's needs for assistance in dressing and toileting, it also increased their dependence on carers. Furthermore, they found that when designing products for people living with dementia and for dementia care, it is essential not to stigmatise the person. They argue that textiles designed for this user group should be designed in a way that supports and maintains the daily routines and agency of the person. It should focus on the well-being of the person in care as opposed to efficiency in care provision and care practices. Thus, guidelines and regulations are needed for the use of such products.

In supporting people living with dementia struggling with dysphagia (trouble in swallowing), Casiddu and Porfirione (2017) designed a new hardware/software mobile system to monitor a person's swallowing. Employing a user-centred approach and an interdisciplinary team of clinicians, industrial designers, and engineers they developed a system that will help patients with dysphagia deal with their rehabilitation at home, safely and autonomously. Their approach and design feature a suitable and ergonomic design, taking into consideration the psychological repercussions on users and how easily they would accept the solutions offered.

On a very different area, Anderiesen et al. (2015) explored which play experiences can be expected to be suitable for persons in different stages of dementia. By reviewing neuroimaging, neuropathological and clinical studies they found that 22 play experiences were related to the neuropathology that is characteristic of the different stages of dementia: earliest, mild-to-moderate and severe. Their research provides guidelines for game developers to design games for persons with Alzheimer's Disease that contribute to a meaningful and fun way of spending their time. They also suggest that games should be designed to match the players' cognitive abilities, which are also challenging and stimulating.

Moving into work on design research methods within the context of dementia, we encounter Smeenk's et al. (2017) and Rodgers' (2018) research on the use of co-design. Using a case study involving a dementia simulator, Smeenk's et al. (2017) illustrate how the approach contributes to understanding users, transferring insights and translating empathy into design. Their proposal addresses three sequential co-design activities facilitated by an empathic principal designer, namely individual harvest meetings, collective handover workshops and empathic ideation workshops. The positive evaluation of the co-design tool revealed that the approach did not only guide the design team, by offering a practical and coherent process, but also enabled individual team members to be receptive, inclusive and committed to people living with dementia. In another project, Rodgers (2018) worked collaboratively with over 130 people living with dementia across Scotland in the co-design and development of a new tartan. The research resulted in a number of co-designed interventions that will help change the perception of dementia by showing that people living with dementia can offer much to society after diagnosis. Moreover, it is envisaged that the co-designed activities and interventions will help reconnect people recently diagnosed with dementia to help build their self-esteem, identity and dignity and help keep the person living with dementia connected to their community, thus delaying the need for formal support and avoid the need for crisis responses. A number of recommendations for researchers when co-designing with people living with dementia was also developed as a result of the research.

A different design research method was explored by Kenning (2018). Following a Reciprocal Design approach, it provided opportunities for social engagement, interaction with objects and activities, and entertainment for people living with dementia and stakeholders in their care. The study also showed that participants living with dementia, who were not able to verbally articulate likes and dislikes, could communicate in different ways, which included unexpectedly moving around to engage with prototypes or objects with which they had become fascinated, or laughing and smiling as they engaged for sustained periods of time. Designers engaged in the project reported that they benefitted from the experience by being provided with a range of background knowledge to support the design process, and that it has impacted on subsequent design consulting and projects that they have since undertaken. Furthermore, the approach employed helped to change participating designers' perception about people living with dementia and their abilities.

Lastly, Darby and Tsekleves (2018) participatory design fictions to explore the future implications of UK dementia policy. Through a series of codesign workshops they developed a design fiction, conceived by a participant group to provide policy debate. This enabled them to investigate a method to explore and critique possible futures at the intersection of technological advancement and government health policy. Their key focus was on how best to engage people living with dementia but also dementia experts in design fiction as a participatory practice. Their findings and recommendations suggest that slower, more expansive design fiction interventions around health policy are needed to give space for people of diverse abilities and experience to explore and imagine futures afresh. Their research also suggests that affirmative and critical diegetic prototypes may shape the discursive space around policy differently, a possibility that requires further investigation

Conclusion

Drawing on the relevant design research literature this chapter charts the non-pharmacological interventions which have been developed by design researchers exploring different aspects in the context of dementia. Working for and with people living with dementia, several of the interventions design researchers have focused can be grouped into four main themes: reminiscence and personhood; social interaction and living in the moment; independent and assisted living; and cognitive and physical stimulation. These interventions have aimed to support people living with dementia and their informal and formal caregivers in different aspects of their dementia journey. Most of them focus on developing personalised interventions that support positive emotions and activities that foster independence but also social interaction, focusing on the person rather than the disease.

The type of interventions designed were very diverse, ranging from: engaging different senses through physical and/or physical-digital objects (Oven and Predan, 2015; Kenning and Treadaway, 2018), memory stimulation interventions (Murko and Kunze, 2015; Pedro et al., 2015), engaging and stimulation social interaction through music (Favilla and Pedell, 2013; Morrissey et al., 2016; Müller-Rakow and Flechtner, 2017), digital tools for art therapy (Michailidis et al., 2010), interior design and architecture modification to provide more independence for people living with dementia (van Hoof et al., 2013; Van der Linden et al., 2016), developing assistive technology systems to support people living with dementia and carers throughout the course of dementia (Hattink, et al., 2016), physical and cognitive stimulation through video games and traditional tangible games (Tobiasson et al.,

2015; King and Siu, 2017); the design of playful artefacts for cognitive and physical stimulation for people living with late-stage dementia in residential care (Treadaway et al., 2016) and several others.

In doing so design researchers have employed and often adapted existing design research methodologies (such as design ethnography, participatory design, etc.) in order to accommodate working in the context of dementia. More importantly, design researchers sought ways to ensure wider participation of people living with dementia in the design process of interventions and research.

References

Anderiesen, H., Scherder, E., Goossens, R., Visch, V. and Eggermont, L. (2015). Play experiences for people with Alzheimer's disease. *International Journal of Design*, 9 (2): 155–165.

Branco, R. M., Quental, J. and Ribeiro, Ó. (2017). Personalised participation: an approach to involve people with dementia and their families in a participatory design project. *CoDesign*, 13 (2): 127–143.

Brankaert, R. G. A. and de Jong, H. J. (2015, July). "A Point in the Right Direction: A Simple Navigation Device for People with Dementia." In *Third European Conference on Design4health*, pp. 1–9, 13–16 July 2015, Sheffield, UK.

Braun, V. and Clarke, V. (2006). Using thematic analysis in psychology. *Qualitative Research in Psychology*, 3 (2): 77–101.

Casiddu, N. and Porfirione, C. (2017). Design for dysphagia: a new hardware-and-software mobile system to monitor patients' swallowing. *The Design Journal*, 20 (sup1): S2078–S2089

Darby, A. G. and Tsekleves, E. (2018). "Mentian: Developing Design Fiction for Dementia Policy." In *Proceedings of the Design Research Society Conference 2018: Design Research Society Conference Proceedings 2018*, pp. 2407–2421. Limerick: Design Research Society.

Favilla, S. and Pedell, S. (2013, November). "Touch Screen Ensemble Music: Collaborative Interaction for Older People with Dementia." In *Proceedings of the 25th Australian Computer-Human Interaction Conference: Augmentation, Application, Innovation, Collaboration*, pp. 481–484. New York: Association for Computing Machinery.

Garde, J. A., Van Der Voort, M. C. and Niedderer, K. (2018). "Design Probes for People with Dementia." In *Proceedings of the Design Research Society Conference 2018: Design Research Society Conference Proceedings 2018*, pp. 2607–2621. Limerick: Design Research Society.

Gowans, G., Dye, R., Alm, N., Vaughan, P., Astell, A. and Ellis, M. (2007). Designing the interface between dementia patients, caregivers and computer-based intervention. *The Design Journal*, 10 (1): 12–23.

Hanson, E., Magnusson, L., Arvidsson, H., Claesson, A., Keady, J. and Nolan, M. (2007). Working together with persons with early stage dementia and their family members to design a user-friendly technology-based support service. *Dementia*, 6 (3): 411–434.

Hattink, B. J. J., Meiland, F. J. M., Overmars-Marx, T., de Boer, M., Ebben, P. W. G., van Blanken, M., Verhaeghe, S., Stalpers-Croeze, I., Jedlitschka, A., Flick, S. E., v/

d Leeuw, J., Karkowski, I. and Droes, R. M. (2016). The electronic, personalizable Rosetta system for dementia care: exploring the user-friendliness, usefulness and impact. *Disability and Rehabilitation: Assistive Technology*, 11 (1): 61–71.

Iltanen-Tähkävuori, S., Wikberg, M. and Topo, P. (2012). Design and dementia: a case of garments designed to prevent undressing. *Dementia*, 11 (1): 49–59.

Jakob, A. and Collier, L. (2017). Sensory enrichment for people living with dementia: increasing the benefits of multisensory environments in dementia care through design. *Design for Health*, 1 (1): 115–133.

Kenning, G. (2018). Reciprocal design: inclusive design approaches for people with late stage dementia. *Design for Health*, 2 (1): 1–21

Kenning, G. and Treadaway, C. (2018). Designing for dementia: iterative grief and transitional objects. *Design Issues*, 34 (1): 42–53.

King, A. P. Y. and Siu, K. W. M. (2017). Participant observation in cognitive gameplay as a rehabilitation tool for living alone elderly with dementia in Hong Kong: a pilot study. *The Design Journal*, 20 (sup1): S2426–S2438.

Lazar, A., Thompson, H. and Demiris, G. (2014). A systematic review of the use of technology for reminiscence therapy. *Health Education & Behavior*, 41 (1_ suppl): 51S–61S.

Mihailidis, A., Blunsden, S., Boger, J., Richards, B., Zutis, K., Young, L. and Hoey, J. (2010). Towards the development of a technology for art therapy and dementia: definition of needs and design constraints. *The Arts in Psychotherapy*, 37 (4): 293–300.

Morrissey, K., Wood, G., Green, D., Pantidi, N. and McCarthy, J. (2016, June). "'I'm a Rambler, I'm a Gambler, I'm a Long Way from Home' The Place of Props, Music, and Design in Dementia Care." In *Proceedings of the 2016 ACM Conference on Designing Interactive Systems*, pp. 1008–1020. New York: Association for Computing Machinery.

Müller-Rakow, A. and Flechtner, R. (2017). Designing interactive music systems with and for people with dementia. *The Design Journal*, 20 (sup1): S2207–S2214

Murko, P. and Kunze, C. (2015). "Tangible Memories: Exploring the Use of Tangible Interfaces for Occupational Therapy in Dementia Care." In *Proceedings of the 3rd European Conference on Design4Health* (Vol. 13, p. 16).

Oven, P. Č. and Predan, B. (2015). "A Set of Social Games for Senior Citizens with Dementia/D9." In *Proceedings of the 3rd European Conference on Design4Health*, pp. 1–11, Sheffield, UK, 13–16 July 2015.

Pedro, M., Costa, A. and Lopes, L. (2015). "Dementia – Stimulation of Memories." In *Third European Conference on Design4health*, 13–16 July 2015, Sheffield, UK.

Rodgers, P. A. (2018). Co-designing with people living with dementia. *CoDesign*, 14 (3): 188–202.

Smeenk, W., Sturm, J. and Eggen, B. (2017). Empathic handover: how would you feel? Handing over dementia experiences and feelings in empathic co-design. *CoDesign*, 14 (4): 1–16.

Snyder, C. (2003). Paper prototyping: The fast and easy way to design and refine user interfaces. San Francisco: Morgan Kaufmann.

Subramaniam, P. and Woods, B. (2010). Towards the therapeutic use of information and communication technology in reminiscence work for people with dementia: a systematic review. *International Journal of Computers in Healthcare*, 1 (2): 106–125.

Tobiasson, H., Sundblad, Y., Walldius, Å. and Hedman, A. (2015). Designing for active life: moving and being moved together with dementia patients. *International Journal of Design*, 9 (3): 47–62.

Treadaway, C., Prytherch, D., Kenning, G. and Fennell, J. (2016). "In the Moment: Designing for Late Stage Dementia." In *Proceedings of DRS2016: Design+ Research+ Society-Future-Focused Thinking* (Vol. 8). London: Design Research Society.

Treadaway, C., Taylor, A. and Fennell, J. (2019). Compassionate design for dementia care. *International Journal of Design Creativity and Innovation*, 7 (3): 144–157.

van Hoof, J., Blom, M. M., Post, H. N. and Bastein, W. L. (2013). Designing a "Think-Along Dwelling" for people with dementia: a co-creation project between health care and the building services sector. *Journal of Housing for the Elderly*, 27 (3): 299–332.

Van der Linden, V., Van Steenwinkel, I., Dong, H. and Heylighen, A. (2016, June). "Designing 'Little Worlds' in Walnut Park: How Architects Adopted an Ethnographic Case Study on Living with Dementia." In *Proceedings of DRS2016: Design Research Society-Future-Focused Thinking* (Vol. 8, pp. 3199–3212). London: Design Research Society.

Woods, R. T., Orrell, M., Bruce, E., Edwards, R. T., Hoare, Z., Hounsome, B., Keady, J., Moniz-Cook, E., Orgeta, V., Rees, J. and Russell, I. T. (2016). REMCARE: pragmatic multi-centre randomised trial of reminiscence groups for people with dementia and their family carers: effectiveness and economic analysis. *PLoS ONE*, 11 (4): e0152843.

Part 2

Case studies

Case study 1

Name: Open Doors: The changing face of our neighbourhood
Lead: Caroline Swarbrick
Theme: Reminiscence and personhood
Approach/method: Co-design/participatory
Location: Salford, UK

Case study details

This case study was part of the Neighbourhoods and Dementia Study (2014–2019), which is a large, multi-centre international study on neighbourhoods and dementia (Keady et al., 2014; https://sites.manchester.ac.uk/neighbourhoods-and-dementia/; accessed 20 August 2020). Funded by the Economic and Social Research Council (ESRC)/National Institute for Health Research (NIHR).

The project started with Open Doors in 2014. Open Doors is a very big network, which started as peer support and post-diagnostic support, but it has grown and evolved into different types of groups to support people living with dementia (i.e. dog-walking group, book-reading group, etc).

Since the project was part of the wider Neighbourhoods and Dementia study, it revolved around neighbourhoods. In the first discussion the group had posed the question: '*What does the term "neighbourhoods" mean to you?*' and, '*This is where we are now.*' From that conversation, it was clear that there were a lot of shared experiences that people had not talked about before, because there was no forum to do that.

The focus was on regeneration and about how community and neighbourhoods had changed. Within the Salford context, where this study took place, it was split into neighbourhoods, so it had different connotations, but it was very much in terms of how those neighbourhoods and people that had experienced those neighbourhoods had broken up and fragmented for several different reasons. Because of that fragmentation, it impacted on so much – on work patterns, on family, on where people lived, the introduction of high-rise flats, how people understood and experienced those changes and how it shapes them today.

Over the course the project engaged with about 45 people, co-researchers, people living with dementia, with and without capacity, and family. The project team also included an existing facilitator, who knew the group on a very individual basis, and a clinical psychologist to also cater for independent support.

Research method

A participatory research approach (Satcher, 2005) was employed along with cooperative inquiry (Reason, 1994). It should be mentioned that cooperative inquiry has not been used widely in the field of dementia.

Typically, cooperative inquiry brings together people who did not previously know each other. However, that was not appropriate for this type of study and as such it was unknown at the project start what the outcomes would be.

One of the project aims was to take participatory research within this context, beyond Patient and Public Involvement (PPI) and embrace the feedback that people feel quite involved tokenistically.

The project was set up as an Open Doors research group. From the start of the project, the research team's role changed from that of decision maker to taking a real back step, focusing mainly on facilitating and focusing research. The following quote is characteristic of the ethos of the project:

> We want to do this research project, but the rest of it is down to you. You tell me what you want to do and I'll be here to try and make that happen for you.
> (Interviewee)

Although the project started gradually, the initial meetings were crucial as they set what the expectations were of each other and were employed to put together a list of shared communication. This was a list of words that the research team would use and will not use, so that everyone was very clear and there were no misunderstandings.

The study defined collectively the focus and vision, which was learning about new skills but about challenging as well; about challenging others and challenging the group itself.

The project included two studies. In the first study, the group wanted to do some filming talk about how regeneration has impacted them. It was very much that people wanted that visual. It's so important because, as well, it engages people who may not be able to articulate or recall certain aspects. Dementia came out, but it very much came from the individuals. It was not the focus, and even though everybody was there because of dementia in whatever capacity, that was underlying. People could bring it out as and when it was.

The research team introduced archived footage and photographs. They met several times at the Salford Art Gallery and Museum, which has a great archive about the city. Within the art gallery, people could just go, look and reflect. The group had so much fun just going through the archive. Some of them triggered a lot of memories that you do not ordinarily remember, but when you see it, it generated rich discussions in a different way.

The art gallery and museum has memory boxes, some of which were loaned to the group to explore. People donate to the boxes, and there were a couple of photographs that people actually recognised either by themselves or by their family members. Several people from the group also donated some of their own items to go in the boxes for other people to share as well.

For the filming, the group worked with somebody from the BBC, who also produces films for people living with dementia, and was thus acutely aware of the different types of needs, of engaging with people. They produced three films of over 10 hours of footage.

After the film was launched, instead of simply archiving it, the group decided to produce some animations from it – in order to transfer their experiences and their understandings to the next generation.

A local animation company, which previously had also worked with people living with dementia, produced several animations, which again were led by the group. They made all the key decisions, developed the script and built it iteratively by offering their feedback.

With regards to the study evaluation, it was noted that the group did not want a formal evaluation, as it felt that it was not a natural part of the group meetings. Instead, the team decided to explore this differently by focusing on how they would evaluate their own learning as opposed to formally evaluating the study. This resulted in an ongoing 'creative' evaluation, which included consent to take photographs and videos and use quotes that people have used across the board.

Lessons learnt

Several lessons were learnt and questions were raised by the case study.

People living with dementia had only ever been involved as participants, therefore being involved in all of the decision making and most of the research process it challenged their perception and that of the research team but also the ethics.

With regards to the former and from the group perspective, research had previously been perceived as being dull and most people's experience were as participants. Therefore, challenging their own perceptions of what research is given that this study was done in a completely different way had its own challenges on a research level, but culturally as well.

From a researcher and research perspective, there seems to be blurring in the literature as co-research/participatory research and PPI are sometimes used interchangeable. Examples include projects in which although people are presented as co-researchers, they are in fact simply the subject of research, often being just interviewed. This in turn creates confusion to people living with dementia who participate in such research studies and it raises questions as to what we need to do as researchers to change our practices to truly involve people in research as co-researchers (Swarbrick et al., 2019).

Regarding ethics, co-researching with people living with dementia raises challenges at different levels. At one level, as researchers it is critical to engage with groups of people living with dementia prior to the start of the research study in order to develop familiarity and trust, which is essential. However, this means that as ethics approval is not always certain one has to manage the group expectations and be transparent right from the start that one might not get approval to do co-design research.

Given the novelty of application of co-research/co-design research methodology within this context, ethics committees may often not fully recognise the research element of the study and, as in the case of this study, misjudge it as being *'just about engagement, about social responsibility'*. The research team was faced by questions of *'where's the science?'* and *'where are your measures?'* Which was followed by response that *'the science is in the methodology'* and *'we're not doing formal measures'*

The aforementioned demonstrates that we are still very constrained within our own research culture and the ethics to conduct this type of research, as there is often no consistency between them. Therefore, challenging our own peers' perception of methodologies within the context of dementia research studies is challenging, but one way of moving forward.

With regards to research methods, it was also highlighted that the literature review on cooperative inquiry, conducted at the start of this study, indicated a diverse way of involving people into research projects. As the research team employed a cooperative inquiry, which had not been used in the field of dementia before, it needed adapting. This was a key learning process for the research team as well as all the members of the group.

One of the difficulties that the research team is starting to face at the moment, which they knew was coming, is that expectations are just raised and everybody is so engaged. The challenge lies in how to draw an end to the project. At the time of the interview the research team was working with the psychologist to see how they can best manage this. This is a challenge that all projects involving either research participants or co-researchers, especially within the context of dementia face (Escalante et al., 2017).

Additional lessons learnt also include working with an established group for this type of projects, and not being too prescribed about the specific activities. Provided there is focus and clarity, activities can be amended as the project proceeds. Giving people choice and opportunity helps in learning new skills and for people to challenge others, and to be challenged. This also challenges researchers, resulting in asking questions about what their own research agenda and their priorities were. The project that the team came out with, would not have been possible of being perceived had it not followed that process. As the project lead indicates:

Often as researchers we tend to have our own research ideas with how a project fits in with policy, how it fits in with the objectives, whatever guidelines are there and how everything ties up. Going, asking people, 'Well, actually, what's your priority'" knocks it on the head completely.

(Interviewee)

Furthermore, the research team found that having two facilitators were extremely helpful, in case somebody got distressed. As everybody, especially people living with dementia, have good and bad days, having an extra person there who can say '*Do you want to come out and talk this through?*' means that the research team does not have to stop the group and that the rest of the people do not then get unsettled.

Lastly, an advice to other researchers from this case study is to work, wherever possible, with an established dementia community group and as researchers in this field to challenge our own research agendas and what the real priorities are.

References

Escalante, M. A., Tsekleves, E., Bingley, A. F. and Gradinar, A. I. (2017). Ageing playfully: a story of forgetting and remembering. *Design for Health*, 1 (1): 134–145.

Keady, J., Clark, A., Ferguson-Coleman, E., Helstrom, I., Hyden, L. C., Pendleton, N., Reilly, S., Swarbrick, C., Ward, R. and Young, A. (2014). Neighbourhoods and dementia. *The Journal of Dementia Care*, 22 (6): 16–17.

Reason, P. (1994). "Three Approaches to Participative Inquiry." In N. K. Denzin and Y. S. Lincoln (Eds.), *Handbook of Qualitative Research*, pp. 324–339. Thousand Oaks, CA, : Sage.

Satcher, D. (2005). *Methods in Community-Based Participatory Research for Health*. John Wiley.

Swarbrick, C. M., Doors, O., Scottish Dementia Working Group, EDUCATE, Davis, K. and Keady, J. (2019). Visioning change: co-producing a model of involvement and engagement in research (Innovative Practice). *Dementia*, 18 (7–8): 3165–3172.

Case study 2

Name: MinD: Designing mindful self-empowerment and social engagement
Lead: Kristina Niedderer, Manchester Metropolitan University, UK
Theme: Social interaction and personhood
Approach/method: Co-design/participatory
Location: UK, Germany, Luxemburg, Netherlands, Spain, Italy, Australia and Russia

Case study details

There is an increasing recognition that mindfulness can be helpful to people of all ages, including people living with dementia. There are different approaches to mindfulness, most prominently by Kabat-Zinn (2003) and Langer (1990), and both can be useful. However, both require stimulation or practice, often in the form of a trainer. Design can offer to provide this role in a number of different ways by stimulation attentiveness and reflection (Niedderer, 2014). Design interventions are, however, rarely recognised in relation to reducing stress, anxiety or depression, supporting relationships, or maintaining quality of life, especially in the dementia context. Where they are recognised, it is usually as 'assistive technology', rather than as design (e.g. Guss et al., 2014). The MinD project explored different ways in which mindful design can support people living with dementia with relaxation, self-empowerment, social interaction and engagement.

The project MinD 'Designing for People with Dementia: Designing for mindful self-empowerment and social engagement' was a four-year project funded under the European Horizon 2020, Marie Sklodowska-Curie (MSCA), Research Innovation and Staff Exchange (RISE) programme (2016–2020). It brought together 17 partners from 8 countries, including academic, healthcare, care policy, design and ICT partners from the UK, Germany, Luxembourg, The Netherlands, Spain, Italy, Australia and Russia. This collaborative, multicultural and multidisciplinary team was set perfectly to address complex and global issues relating to dementia. MinD took a design-led approach based on mindful design and co-design, rather than following the typical health or

ICT-led themes, to offer an empathic approach that recognises and supports people living with dementia as individuals (Niedderer, 2017).

Key aims and outputs of the MinD project included: The formal recognition of design as an important means of personal support for people living with dementia, and in the broader health and care context in general (Niedderer et al., 2020). Advice for the inclusion of mindfulness in people's lives through design in the health and care context, in particular for people living with dementia (Dening et al., 2020). The design of three prototypes and their evaluation as demonstrators of supporting people living with dementia through design: The 'Living the Life' reflective booklet, offering simple advice and mindfulness exercises, to help people maintain a positive attitude and control over their lives, following the diagnosis; the 'This is Me' boardgame to help empower people, following the diagnosis, by refocusing on the positives in life, on what they can and want to do, and the hybrid electronic system, 'Let's meet Up!', which aims to help people living with dementia to stay active and socially engaged.

Research method

The project was a complex multidimensional project, employing several different methods across its three phases of data collection, design and evaluation. In the data collection phase, research methods included individual and focus-group interviews with people with early-mid-stage dementia and carers, and visual probes (Garde et al., 2018). The design phase comprised of brainstorming and ideation techniques, participant consultation, concept development and prototype development methods. In addition, co-design methods were used to include people living with dementia directly in the development of the designs (Niedderer et al., 2017; Dening et al., 2020). The evaluation phase emulated the data collection phase. Here the prototypes were presented to people living with dementia in individual or focus group sessions to use the designs, and to feedback on their experience and the usefulness of the designs with regard to well-being, self-empowerment and social engagement as well as mindfulness related aspects. Participants were involved in the study throughout, partly through traditional data collection methods, and partly through public and patient involvement to provide feedback, advice and input on the project work. In particular, through co-design activities, they were involved in the design development from the beginning to the end, including the idea development, decision making, concept development and prototype development stages.

Lessons learnt

There were several lessons to be learnt from this case study. First of all, the research project demonstrated that design can help people living with dementia manage their life better. It can contribute to subjective well-being, agency and self-empowerment as well as offering aspects of enjoyment, conviviality and social connection, in particular, where design is used to instil mindfulness in people's lives. The key benefits of working in this area as designers is in being able to make a substantial contribution to the real world, to improve people's lives and to support people living with dementia in living a better life.

The value of including people living with dementia, carers and professional healthcare staff into the research and design of the prototypes had been considerable. Especially, the comprehensive use of co-design and co-production processes with direct involvement of people living with dementia, have enhanced mutual understandings of the issues at stake and significantly informed the design development.

The advice for researchers wishing to work with people living with dementia is to include them if possible from the very beginning and throughout the project, ensuring a meaningful and equitable role beyond that of mere 'research subjects'. Although engaging caregivers and care professional is also beneficial, only people living with dementia really know what it feels like to live with dementia and what can help them.

A challenge in this project has been dealing with the ethical requirements for research, especially in the UK. When dealing with people living with dementia, who are classed as 'vulnerable people', ethics requirements tend to assume a clinical approach, which is often not appropriate for a design study. This adds unnecessarily to the workload and adds obstacles to conducting this kind of work. While people living with dementia need to be protected, it should not hinder designers and people living with dementia to meet and to deny people living with dementia important opportunities. A more differentiated and informed approach to ethics in relation to the creative disciplines therefore is needed.

Acknowledgements

The MinD project has received funding from the European Union's Horizon 2020 research and innovation programme under the Marie Skłodowska-Curie grant agreement No 691001. University of Wolverhampton is the project co-ordinator with the following partners: Nottinghamshire Healthcare NHS Trust, UK; Manchester Metropolitan University, UK; Etic Lab, UK; Alzheimer Europe ASBL, LU; Université du Luxembourg, LU; Universiteit Twente, NL; Zorggroep Sint Maarten, NL; Panton BV, NL; Technische Universitaet Dresden, DE; Alexianer St. Hedwig Kliniken Berlin GmbH, DE; Fundación INTRAS, ES; Picharchitects, ES; Universitat Politècnica de Catalunya, ES; Fundació Eurecat, ES; DUIT srl, IT; Queensland University of Technology, Australia; ITMO University, RU. Kristina Niedderer, the project Principal Investigator, has supplied the information for the case study. For more information on the project visit: www.designingfordementia.eu

References

Dening, T., Gosling, J., Craven, M. and Niedderer, K. (2020). *Guidelines for Designing with and for People with Dementia*. MinD & Project Partners. https://designingfordementia.eu/resources/publications

Garde, J. A., Van Der Voort, M. C., and Niedderer, K. (2018). "Design Probes for People with Dementia. " In *Proceedings of DRS 2018: Design as a Catalyst for Change*, pp. 2607–2621, 2. Limerick.

Guss, R., Middleton, J., Beanland, T., Slade, L., Moniz-Cook, E., Watts, S. and Bone, A. (2014). *A Guide to Psychosocial Interventions in Early Stages of Dementia*. Leicester, UK: The British Psychological Society.

Kabat-Zinn, J. (2003). Mindfulness-based interventions in context: past, present, and future. *Clinical Psychology: Science and Practice*, 10 (2): 144–156.

Langer, E. (1990). *Mindfulness*. Cambridge, MA: DACapo Press.

Niedderer, K., Dening, T. and Powell, K. (2020). *Recognising Design as a Means for Enhancing Quality of Life, Self-Empowerment and Social Engagement for People with Dementia*. Mind Recommendations for Funders & Policymakers, Designers, Design Researchers & Design Educators, Design Regulators & Voluntary Organisations, MinD & project partners. https://designingfordementia.eu/resources/publications

Niedderer, K., Tournier, I., Coleston-Shields, D., Craven, M., Gosling, J., Garde, J. A., Bosse, M., Salter, B. and Griffoen, I. (2017). "Designing with and for People with Dementia: Developing a Mindful Interdisciplinary Co-Design Methodology." In *Proceedings of the IASDR International Conference 2017*. Cincinnati, USA, 31October-3 November 2017. doi: 10.7945/C2G67F.

Niedderer, K., & Townsend, K. (2014). Designing craft research: Joining emotion and knowledge. The Design Journal, 17(4), 624-647.

Case study 3

Name: Care-Wear: Garments for people living with dementia in care homes
Lead: Minttu Wikberg
Theme: Independent and assisted living
Approach/method: User-centred
Location: Helsinki, Finland

Case study details

This case study explored branding and the image of old age, looking at ways of improving it. The underlying strategy involved looking at how we deal with brands, marketing and brand images in commercial settings, and seeing what we can learn and transfer from those to render the image of old age more positive, and the way that people feel about old age.

Focusing on hygiene overalls used in care environments in Finland by people living with dementia was one of the products the case study explored. The underlying aim was to develop a garment that would meet not only the functional needs related to dementia and incontinence, but also the expressive needs of the wearer (Wikberg, 2008).

Hygiene overalls refer to specially designed garments that make it difficult for the wearer to undress on their own, in order to prevent people with cognitive decline to undress in socially inappropriate situations. Hygiene overalls present an interesting area of study in relation to clothing and old age in a care setting. This is because on one hand clothes are a way of communicating social roles and personal identities and on the other hand, the link between clothing and dementia has rarely gained the attention of researchers and fashion designers (Iltanen-Tähkävuori et al., 2012).

Research method

The research approach included human-centred methods, such as observations and interviews. The research team interviewed the staff at the dementia care facility, in order to gain knowledge and hands-on information about the different aspects of dementia care and specifically the patient overalls. Observations of the dementia care facility and of the people living in it were conducted, to develop a better understanding of the context and challenges people living with dementia faced with it. In addition to this, one of the design researchers also employed knowledge gained in her previous occupation as a nurse of how, for example, patients are when they are unable to clothe them-selves, and how the nurses put the clothes on.

Analysis of the findings revealed that there is need for a new version of the patient overall for people living with dementia, which:

- Enables the wearer to express femininity or masculinity, and their own personal dress style
- Is functional but also aesthetically pleasing, not being visually stigma-tizing for the wearer or making visible their dementia or incontinence problems

This led to the design of a new garment (named Care-Wear) aimed at lessening some of the problems associated with the current patient overall. The garment, which is 95 percent bamboo and five percent lycra fibres, looks like a normal two-piece outfit, incorporating the functional solutions needed. More precisely, since both the upper and the bottom parts can be separated, it allows more ways of combining the pieces to create different styles, colour combinations and either more feminine or masculine styles. The bottom part (trousers) can be attached to the upper garment by means of a horizontal zipper, to make the outfit a one-piece suit.

The new garment design was evaluated at the care home facility. The care home personnel evaluated what it was like to put on, how robust and easy it was to care for it (i.e. washing), as overalls needs to last for several years, due to their costs. It was also evaluated with one person living with dementia in the care facility. Although she was not verbal anymore, she was able to select the designs she wanted from the images of the clothes, with different colours and prints the research team showed her.

Lessons learnt

Three main elements of discussion emerge from the case study.

The first relates to the value of design within this context. More precisely, designing for people living with dementia demonstrates inclusiveness and respect for people who cannot ask for it, and who are, maybe, frail and fragile. It relates to essentials consumer goods, such as clothing, which all enjoy. This is currently reflected in the original design of patient overalls, which are based on the needs as expressed by carers, not by the people wearing them.

The use of hygiene overall benefits family carers and care staff by making it possible to control the wearer's needs for assistance in dressing and toileting. This, however, increases the dependence of the person living with dementia on their caregivers. Furthermore, such products also communicate the wearers' fragility and that they are currently in formal/informal care. This raises an ethical dilemma concerning use. On one hand, it can be claimed to be essential in the care of people living with dementia. On the other hand, the garment is seen as visually stigmatising for the wearer. Also, as these are restrictive garments, questions are raised whether there should always be permission from the patient and how viable that would be for people living with progressive forms of dementia. This necessitates the development of guidelines and regulations for the use of such products.

One of the key outcomes of this case study is to provoke some public discussion about this subject. Because, if we want to be able to offer clothing choices for people living with dementia in care settings, this will result in higher costs. If this is to be paid by governments or other communities, then there should be pressure from the public, for more funds to be directed on these products. In addition to this, there is a need for more designers to engage with research in developing such products. Although it has not been traditionally popular for the design community to design for hospitals and patients, this is currently changing. In particularly, in Finland, there are several start-ups and companies developing applications for mobile phones related to healthcare.

Lastly, one of the key advice from the case study lead is the importance of conducting user-centred research, such as observations prior to the study start, especially if one has limited experience in healthcare. As Minttu Wikberg notes: *'it's also helpful if you're able to observe things as an outsider and then ask questions, like, "Why do you do it like that?" So, yes, I think, at least, you have to really go there and see how things are done and how people live'*.

References

Iltanen-Tähkävuori, S., Wikberg, M., and Topo, P. (2012). Design and dementia: a case of garments designed to prevent undressing. *Dementia*, 11 (1): 49–59.

Wikberg, M. (2008). Vanhuus muokkaa mielikuvia. Master's Theses. Helsinki: Taideteollinen korkeakoulu. Helsinki University of Art and Design.

Case study 4

Name: Collaborative interaction for older people living with dementia through touch screen music
Lead: Stu Favilla and Sonja Pedell
Theme: Social interaction and living in the moment
Approach/method: Co-design/participatory
Location: Melbourne, Australia

Case study details

The music ensemble project explored the role technology can play, in particular to enhance social interactions. The project focused on how one can use technologies to enhance social interaction of people, maintain skills and even look into building new interests, building new experiences. Not just focusing technology on reminiscence and memory, memory training, which have been over explored within this context.

Looking at technologies, such as the iPad, one can see that it has been predominantly used for single use, or to contact someone remotely. In this case study, the research team explored how can we use the iPad, but by moving away from having one person in front of it; fostering shared interaction and a social experience.

A council with a rapidly growing population in the west of Melbourne, with a new Ageing Well facility and a group focusing on people living with dementia was selected for this case study. The time people spend within the Ageing Well programme, ranged from half a day to an entire day once a week, or even more days. Positive experiences and outcomes were reported.

Research method

A participatory design process was followed throughout the case study. A process of observations and familiarisation with the environment and people in it took place prior to the start of the co-design process. Several co-design sessions then took place, typically lasting two hours. In each session the research team will engage people living with dementia and get that continuous feedback, develop their knowledge of how much people engaged with the iPads and develop the screen design as well as the interactions. Data was collected in various forms, initially through journaling observations and voluntary interviews, and then by recording iPad gestural control data and video.

The research team worked in context, without a formal process of participant recruitment. They worked with the whole group, as it was there, as that gave them the opportunity to also find out how to compare it. Staff were a really important stakeholder group. They appreciated the research team coming in and bringing these technologies, as tools and support, into their work. They were really good in articulating not only what they saw, the case study contributed to that group, but also what impact it had afterwards. This included continuous testimonies and that people living with dementia engaging in the study were more lively and were less prone to fall to a negative mood towards the afternoon (after the group had left).

In terms of the iPad applications that the research team explored with the people living with dementia several ones, such as using Google Maps to take people who had emigrated to Australia back to their home village in Italy and showing them what the house that they were born in looked like from the street. This made them realise that such apps require a one-on-one carer for persons living with dementia to just walk them through the app. Furthermore, as the Ageing Well group, expanded from 12 persons to 40 now, new models of integrating several people, but without necessarily working with the whole group at once, were required.

The concept of scaffold interaction (Quinn and Wild, 1998; Hearst, 1999) was proposed as a potential solution to that. It has been used with helper teachers that assist children that might have special learning needs. It would allow them to participate in the class, but they would have a one-on-one teacher relationship throughout the course of their day. The research team wanted to explore this concept and extend it within the dynamics of the group of people living with dementia, by having group interactions where there is maybe one person scaffolding four or five people.

Therefore, this was set up to work at a table in a context where there were some people doing another activity, like a jigsaw, or there would be people doing art projects in the same room. At another part of the room there was some music was played on iPad, with two or three people at a time playing in the same interaction.

The research team along with the group of people living with dementia started exploring and playing around with music on the iPad, which included unusual, avant-garde types of synthesiser-based music. The app included sounds that did not have any beats or any pitch, where users could use the whole screen as a X, Y touchpad to set up different things to happen in different areas of the screen. This encouraged people to explore the app and provided them with radical sound outcomes, depending on what they did.

Furthermore, the software allowed them to trace all of the user movements on the iPad screen. This was really useful, as it enabled the research team to see that there was a clear change in the behaviour in the app use. More precisely, the team noticed that several people would come to a new setup, a new sound, to explore and they would move their finger very methodically, at the same speed, usually around the edges of the iPad screen and around the edges of the interaction space. Then, over time, they would move into the centre and they would change their rate, and they would start playing gestures. So, the music became a tool providing them with more and more opportunities for reaction for their interaction.

Also, the software setup use allowed the research team to do rapid prototyping during the co-design sessions. This enabled changes in the actual music sessions and trying different user interfaces. Therefore, each week research team looked at different user interface elements, such as the size of buttons and layout, and how things would work, doing a lot of customisation. They could also make changes to the synthesis and to the ensemble music attributes during the sessions and test quickly. During the iPad testing the team observed that high levels of interaction ranging from 45 to 90 minutes, with some users immersing and reminiscing past experiences related to music.

Lessons learnt

There are several points for discussion and lessons learnt resulting from this case study.

First, there is a recognition that although dementia is medically classed as a terminal disease (Mitchell et al., 2009) people can live 15–20 years with dementia. Therefore, we should start approaching it more as a disability than a terminal disease, and ensure that people can contribute and be part of shared social and meaningful activities aimed at increasing well-being. Approaching dementia from a well-being and quality of life point of view, aside from clinical trials or medical research approach, comes with challenges. Namely, we do have the challenge in articulating, beyond anecdotal evidence, what is the measurable impact on a large scale.

There is currently a considerable amount of research in the area of well-being, but the focus is on the past and reminiscing (Cotelli et al., 2012; Woods et al., 2018). Although it is clear that there are some benefits in reminiscing therapy, there is more opportunity in activating the brain and trying to engage people living with dementia, by introducing them, also, to new things. Specifically, within the context of the impact on connectivity in the neurological pathways, it is in the here and in the now, and in the moment where we should encourage people living with dementia to experience something new. There is often an underestimation of what people can do. The brain is fragmented, but that means there are these fragments who are really up for some amazing things to do. Thus, there is an opportunity to return agency with technology, to restore some sense of agency in these people, and the results of those things are really quite extraordinary.

Secondly, in terms of design, co-design is a potent way to address several of the challenges within the context of dementia and well-being. Nevertheless, researchers, who engage with people living with dementia in longitudinal co-design studies over a year face mortality of participants. This apart from its human aspects raises challenges in gathering of long-term data across one or two years, which is not possible sometimes.

A potential way of mitigating this, is to increase participant sample sizes in co-design studies. However, that provides an enormous amount of work, requiring projects that are exceptionally well resourced. Funding for quality of life and well-being studies is in most case very moderate, hindering this.

Co-design has also received criticism especially in relation to involving people living with moderate and advanced dementia (Hendriks et al., 2015; Tsekleves et al., 2018), as due to their condition they may not be able to directly express view on the design for a product, such as the iPad music app in this case study. This can be mitigated by running several co-design sessions that establish visual and other creative methods for continuous feedback and indirectly building researchers' knowledge, in particular, the interactions into how much people engaged and enjoy with proposed apps, products and the interactions they afford. Moreover, having an extra observer in the field is extremely useful. They can independently observe sessions as well as different groups and provide their overview in debrief session.

Thirdly, in terms of the use of technology within this context, it is important that projects avoid the use of technology as a 'babysitting' tool, as one cannot know what people can really take in. Another aspect to avoid is the conversion of table top games into digital ones, simply because the technology affords to do so. As the interviewee highlighted: '*Why make a game of snakes and ladders on an iPad when there's a beautiful, tactile cardboard game box with a board that's from somebody's grandchildren's collection*'. As there is already a lot of meaning in objects that exist in that space, the aim of technology should be to develop something that integrates well with that space and successfully engage people living with dementia every day.

On top of that and looking at music apps available on iPads, such as the piano apps (i.e. Tiny Piano), these can be discouraging and problematic. On one hand, if one knows how to play piano then it is dissatisfying since it is not really a piano. On the other hand, if one is not able to play an instrument or does not have the skills, they will feel disheartened. Instead, providing an underlying music that people can manipulate can be much more rewarding and encouraging, as they can feel the impact, and produce some of their own music.

In light of this, the look and feel of the apps as well as the output quality and the consistency between the two are very important. For example, apps like the Tiny App, which look like a professional music app with a large list of songs provide the feel of a professional piano. However, the sound output generated sounds like a toy piano. This results again in mismatched expectations and discouragement of using technology for prolonged periods.

On the subject of music and dementia, there is a need for technologies that simply provide a sonic décor inside the living space, such as a residential care facility. This would enable people living with dementia to embrace music into their life but also allow them to have conversations at the same time, without being isolating. This will create a potential for them to be energised and charged up, or calmed down, whilst everyone else in the room do not have to listen to the same soundtrack as well. There are opportunities here for emerging technologies, such as the Internet of Things (Tan and Wang, 2010) and Bone conductor headphones (Atsumi et al., 2006). The former can transform everyday objects, such as lamps in the room into ad hoc music hot spots that are activated automatically or manually. Bone conductor headphones sit in front of one's ears and not over the ears, conducting sound through the bone by vibrating it. Therefore, again they can provide a personalised interaction whilst the person also interacts or sits within a larger group.

Lastly, one observation from the case study was that people living with dementia are great testers. Their unconventional ways of interacting with technology means that they can find an issue or 'bug' (as known in the technology industry) quicker than anyone. For instance, in the case of the iPad interaction, people living with dementia will place their fingers and hands all over the screen. So, as a designer one has to accept that and to reward it in the interaction development.

References

Atsumi, T., Fukuda, M. and Kobayashi, K. (2006). *U.S. Patent No. 7,076,077.* Washington, DC: U.S. Patent and Trademark Office.

Cotelli, M., Manenti, R. and Zanetti, O. (2012). Reminiscence therapy in dementia: a review. *Maturitas*, 72 (3): 203–205.

Hearst, M. A. (1999). "Modern Information Retrieval." In Baeza-Yates, R. and Ribeiro-Neto, B. (Eds.). *User Interfaces and Visualization.* pp. 257–323. Reading MA: Addison Wesley Longman.

Hendriks, N., Slegers, K. and Duysburgh, P. (2015). Codesign with people living with cognitive or sensory impairments: a case for method stories and uniqueness. *CoDesign*, 11 (1): 70–82.

Quinn, C. N. and Wild, M. (1998). Supporting cognitive design: lessons from human-computer interaction and computer-mediated learning. *Education and Information Technologies*, 3 (3–4): 175–185.

Mitchell, S. L., Teno, J. M., Kiely, D. K., Shaffer, M. L., Jones, R. N., Prigerson, H. G., Volicer, L., Givens, J. L. and Hamel, M. B. (2009). The clinical course of advanced dementia. *New England Journal of Medicine*, 361 (16): 1529–1538.

Tan, L. and Wang, N. (2010). "Future Internet: The Internet of Things." In *2010 3rd international conference on advanced computer theory and engineering (ICACTE)* (Vol. 5, pp. V5–376). Chengdu, China: IEEE.

Tsekleves, E., Bingley, A. F., Luján Escalante, M. A. and Gradinar, A. (2018). Engaging people with dementia in designing playful and creative practices: Co-design or co-creation? *Dementia*, 1471301218791692.

Woods, B., O'Philbin, L., Farrell, E. M., Spector, A. E. and Orrell, M. (2018). Reminiscence therapy for dementia. *Cochrane Database of Systematic Reviews*, 3 (2): 1–35.

Case study 5

Name: Designing leisure products for people living with dementia
Lead: Helma van Rijn and Mariet Schreurs
Theme: Reminiscence and personhood
Approach/method: User-centred
Location: Delft, Netherlands

Case study details

This case study explored how design can connect a group of people living with dementia in a care facility. It explored questions such as 'What are the needs of people with dementia?' 'How can we, as designers, learn from how people with dementia interact with the world, for designing?' 'How can we design for them?'

This led to the development of the 'Chitchatters', a leisure game for a group of people living with dementia in day care centres. The game's aim was to stimulate social interaction among people living with dementia.

The case study lasted for three months and it involved people living with dementia in a day care centre in the Netherlands, as well as their relatives, and care professionals, in order to provide the research team with the necessary insight into the experiences and needs of the target group. People living with mild-to-moderate stages of dementia were included in the study, with the person still living in the community, where they received support from a spouse or a professional caregiver.

Research method

The research team employed user-centred design methods that aimed specifically at 'designing for others' by involving those others as informants or participants in the design process. A number of research methods were employed, such as observations, cultural probes, interviews and context-mapping.

The case study started from visits at a day care centre, embedding the research team along with the professional caregivers. This helped dive into the context of study to explore the challenges and opportunities and map the context.

This involved the design team taking part in activities, such as pouring coffee and tea, facilitating the people to the activity room, helping them with preparing lunch, and joining in conversations about the newspaper. In the case of this study, it enabled the research team to observe directly and familiarise themselves with the people at the day care centre.

The research team identified the theme of helping people living with dementia to interact with each other as a key one to explore. They employed observations as well as cultural probes distributed to informal caregivers in order to identify what they used as triggers to converse with people living with dementia and how these could still be used to have a conversation and stay connected to families with them.

Using the feedback from the caregivers, the design team started to further develop the concept into a prototype. The concept of 'the Chitchatters' game consists of four everyday objects: a television, radio, telephone and a treasure box (van Rijn et al., 2010). The objects were designed with an old-fashioned, 60s appearance, to make them look and feel familiar. The aim was for people living with dementia being able to rely on their previous knowledge on operating a television, radio, telephone or treasure box. Each of the objects triggered memories in their own specific way. For example, the television showed movies or video clips, the radio played music and songs, the telephone 'told' poems, and the treasure box revealed objects for reminiscence and tactile stimulation.

The game operated by placing the four objects in a circle around people in the day care centre. A lamp was placed next to each one of the objects as a visual cue, so that once the light was randomly on, the group would focus and interact with that specific object.

The game's software was developed by a professional company in Netherlands. The working prototype of 'the Chitchatters' was tested with a group of 12 people at the day care. In a later stage, researchers evaluated the game in an observation study as people living with dementia engaged with it over a period of time (Nijhof et al., 2013).

Lessons learnt

Conducting research in a day care centre posed challenges for the research team, especially in developing a sustained engagement with the professional caregiver staff. The main reason behind this was the lack of available time care professionals could take to dedicate time to the research team. As the interviewee notes *'it was easy for us to go along providing care, but it was difficult for the care professionals to step into what we wanted to know'*. There were not enough personnel to take care of the people. For instance, when the research team was doing an interview during work time, they had to help people use the toilet, etc.

It was found very difficult to get an in-depth conversation started during their shift. The research team, though, did managed to find other ways to collect data. The use of a diary worked very well. A number of prompting questions were written on the front page, such as what makes people living with dementia happy, etc. Care professionals used the diary, during their coffee break, to respond to the prompting questions.

This is a space where designers along with meaningful design can step in and provide some much needed support for care professionals in day care centres, such as in the case of the Tovertafel product (Anderiesen, 2017), which engages people living with dementia, brings moments of happiness and thus reducing care needs at that moment. Also, a change in the current system and all the legislation and tasks that municipalities ask is required, in order to reduce administration time, freeing more time for care provision.

However, most care professionals or care institutions do not have the investment in innovation and to produce new products. Bringing designers to innovate and produce new products required funding, either from research or from the industry. Opportunities exist, nevertheless, to train care professionals in design research methods and innovation, as this would enable the development of new product ideas, directly from the source. Here subsidies along with start-ups can help drive this field in innovation.

Looking back at the research method of the cultural probe (Gaver et al., 1999), the design team concluded that they had made the questions too confronting by asking about a person's dementia in too focused a way. This led to a very low return of completed probes. A less confronting approach might have been able to gather the required information and the history of people participating in the study. This provided the research team with an important lesson. Namely, to take into account, when designing research tools, not only to the feelings of the people living with dementia, but also pay special attention of how to communicate with their family caregivers.

In the context of dementia, design researchers have several advantages they can contribute. They are very good at exploring new things and at visualising and prototyping. Also, they are able to explore and develop new interventions that enable people living with dementia to interact in new ways with their environment and peers, that can engage them beyond relying solely on verbal communication. Nevertheless, there are specific challenges for design researchers working in this area.

Like with any new user group, one is usually hesitant to start their first engagement. Whilst some researchers are quick and keen to dive into a new world, not everyone is like that. Typically, design researchers engaging with people living with dementia for the first time, take a longer to take the first step and approach their user group. Often due to uncertainty about the unknown and lack of experience in engaging with such user groups.

There is no substitute for engaging with people living with dementia, as it is extremely valuable to see what happens and what the struggles are and to experience that oneself yourself, instead of relying on literature on the subject. Another possibility would be to relate to any past experience that may relate even loosely. For example, one interviewee employed her past experience of working with children with autism, to take that first step and reflect on the lessons learnt from that.

References

Anderiesen, H. (2017). Playful Design for Activation: co-designing serious games for people with moderate to severe dementia to reduce apathy. doi: 10.4233/uuid:ebeef0fa-46fe-4947-86c1-c765a583770a.

Gaver, B., Dunne, T. and Pacenti, E. (1999). Design: cultural probes. *Interactions*, 6 (1): 21–29.

Nijhof, N., van Hoof, J., van Rijn, H. and van Gemert-Pijnen, J. E. W. C. (2013). The behavioral outcomes of a technology-supported leisure activity in people with dementia. *Technology and Disability*, 25 (4): 263–273.

van Rijn, H., van Hoof, J. and Stappers, P. J. (2010). Designing leisure products for people with dementia: developing 'the Chitchatters'' game. *American Journal of Alzheimer's Disease & Other Dementias*, 25 (1): 74–89.

Case study 6

Name: "Think-Along Dwelling" for people living with dementia
Lead: Joost van Hoof
Theme: Independent and assisted living
Approach/method: Researcher
Location: Woerden, Netherlands

Case study details

Enabling ageing-in-place through architectural and technological solutions in the home environment is an increasing aim in the developed world. Within this context in the development of dementia, living environments support independence, compensate for declining and vitality, and lower the burden of family care.

The aim of this study was to design a home for people living with dementia that aims to support ageing-in-place that could be used as a demonstration dwelling for training and education. The study dealt with its development and design by focusing on the architectural and interior design, the physical indoor environment and technological solutions connected to the home. The objective was to develop solutions in the built environment that help support assisted daily living for people living with dementia and help improve the behavioural changes in people.

The design process of the dementia demonstration dwelling has shown that it is possible to integrate evidence-based architectural and technological solutions, which support both individuals living with dementia and their caregivers in daily life situations. The main finding of this case study is that retrofitting a house does not need be costly, since it does not require massive structural alternations, such as tearing down walls or removing staircases, etc.

Research method

The design of the dwelling was based on literature research, and focus group sessions with experts in the field of dementia and housing for older adults.

Based on the literature study, a preliminary concept of a dwelling was designed and presented, which was modified as a result of the focus group sessions. The case study also involved the Dutch Alzheimer's Society ambassadors in the creation of a website for home modifications, who also commented on the design on the use of language.

The fundamentals of the design were that it was aimed at people with dementia living together with a spouse. The design was developed in such a way that it would qualify for all the indicators for rental allowance in the Netherlands.

This led to a demonstration dwelling, which was designed so that it could have been built in an ordinary flat or an apartment block or anywhere in the country, using materials and products, which were already available for sale on the marketplace, so that people could buy them directly and immediately (van Hoof et al., 2013; Kort & van Hoof, 2014).

The demonstration has attracted thousands of visitors ranging from people living with dementia with their caregivers, professional caregivers, occupational/caregiver professionals and students. The feedback from all visitors has been collected. Despite not being the primary goal of this demonstration dwelling, it did help in collecting a lot of viewpoints from people who had experience with people living with dementia but also from people living with dementia themselves. This would not have been possible without the demonstration and it helped the research team in improving their design and recommendations, as they could establish common ground in between all feedback received.

Lessons learnt

In the Netherlands, part of government policy is focused on encouraging the building services sector and industry involved in retrofitting houses for older people, in order to support ageing-in-place. Whilst dementia is on the rise all over the world, the building services industry seeks to respond to the new market a demand for retrofitting houses creates.

The demonstration dwelling clearly facilitates the above but also provides inspiration for new design projects. Especially when one needs to retrofit a nursing home or property owned by a social housing association, they can simply visit these demonstration dwellings. One of the key benefits of the dwelling developed in this case study, is that everything that was presented was already for sale on the marketplace, so people could actually buy it.

Several of demonstration dwellings all over Europe include several robotics and advanced technology prototypes. People who visit these get excited by seeing these, but as they are not market-ready and thus cannot be purchased, people become disappointed and disillusioned.

Evidence-based design was an important challenge discussed. Although the literature includes papers in the area of wayfinding, design of floor plans, design of kitchen areas and patterns, which claim to develop solutions based on evidence-based design, this is not always accurate. This is because the evidence-based design is drawn from existing standards, which have, however, been based on young individuals as opposed to people living with dementia or senior citizens, or derived from small-scale studies and case studies. In addition, there are many differences between building cultures and typologies, and the way we design buildings.

When compared to medical sciences, the evidence available in architecture is poorly collected. Several of the studies that have been conducted are methodologically flawed and often poorly executed. For example, there is research that tests household items, in particular for light therapy for people living with dementia. However, no specific information is provided as to the type of lamp (i.e., incandescent, fluorescent, LED), the light spectrum, output, colour temperature and actual exposure to the light source, etc. These are all critical points in developing a robust evidence base. Interdisciplinary research requires specific knowledge from various domains, which need to come together in a single study.

This is why interdisciplinarity is important in this field, in order to learn from each other's domains. Enabling engineers, architects, designers and medical doctors to work together will help them learn from one another. However, this is not always easy especially as experts often find it difficult to step out from their disciplinary domains and embrace new methods, skills, perspectives, as they may not see the value or importance of the knowledge from another domain, or its uniqueness.

A proposed approach to breaking down disciplinary barriers is to immerse experts in different fields. For instance, experts from the domain of architecture could give up architecture and work in a nursing home for a year, or half a year, or volunteer during the weekends to develop experience and empathy for the people. Since one cannot design for a group of people that one has never encountered, has never engaged with, and have never worked with in the first place. Similarly, for professionals coming from the field of medical or psychological sciences, learning about what encompasses the design process, and that gathering evidence in this field is different from gathering evidence in their own specific fields would be a very useful exercise.

Moreover, it is important for designers and architects to have a good understanding of costs of the measures they propose. For example, how much things actually cost in practice, how finances work in practice, how long the payback time for a new building actually is and who is paying for it (the insurance, the municipality, the social housing association, or private investors). If they know how such financial schemes actually work in practice it is then much easier to work with social housing associations, because you know exactly their boundaries for operation, for making decisions. Too often architects develop great ideas, which cannot be realised, because they do not fit within the financial framework of a housing society. Therefore, learning about budgeting and finance are core skills that especially architects should develop.

A really important point highlighted is that the majority of people living with dementia are not wheelchair users. Therefore, the elements that would help them or should support them in daily living have nothing to do with the building being accessible or not. Furthermore, professionals designing for people living with dementia often only focus on the forgetfulness, or the cognition, and do not account for the problems people face with their activities of daily living (ADL) and behavioural changes.

Looking at the lists of available home modifications and technology interventions for people living with dementia, the vast majority of these measures focus on cognition. Ranging from digital prompts and reminders to picture frames that display date and time. Also measures focusing on, for example, changing the layout of a kitchen, and all the drawers, and putting things in a logical place and regrouping furniture, are aimed at stimulating cognition or support cognition, instead of ADL or with behaviour.

The use of the words 'Think-Along Dwelling', in this case study, focus on the overall aim, that the house can be supportive for people living with dementia. As mentioned by one of the study participants who lives with dementia: *'even though I have dementia I can still think for myself, but I want something to help me memorise'*. And they came up with the 'Think-Along Dwelling' name for the project. Expressing a desire for the house to think along with them and help them find their way around the house. This is a more positive approach to house design, as it does not focus on negativity or on stigma, but the house simply thinks along with its tenant/owner.

In light of this, a key aspect when you design a house for people living with dementia, is that it is not about spending a lot of money. It's about downsizing. It is about designing low-budget solutions that actually help in practice and do not require the help of architects. Things that one can actually do yourself, such as rearranging furniture, putting up curtains, removing locks from certain doors. It can be done by family caregivers or relatives with a very low budget, as most of the demand is on effort and time instead of financial resources.

There is a perception, at least in the Netherlands, that if you want to redesign a house for people living with dementia it would require a significant cost. As this case study has demonstrated, it does not have to cost a lot.

Apart from significant architectural intervention, such as knocking down walls, technology is another element that adds significantly to a budget. However, installing state-of-the-art technology in the home is not needed, since many people today own a smartphone, including people living with dementia. As home automation systems or smart home technologies are becoming quickly obsolete, following the rapid advancement of the pace of innovation they should be taken out. Most of these functionalities can be replaced by a smartphone, which is far more economical and easier to replace.

Lastly, a concern is raised about being able to reproduce what others have done and just gathering enough data to get one work up in the pyramid of evidence. The challenge is that as every single building is a unique design, it is very difficult to compare buildings with one another and to precisely measure the effects of one's design solutions. Gathering the evidence that is robust that can be reused by architects and constructors all over the world forms a great challenge.

On top of that, one should also take into account the fact that building or designing is always based on national standards, cultures and traditions. Like, for instance, in the UK a building having wallpaper in their bathrooms and carpet. In the Netherlands this is not allowed in nursing homes for hygiene purposes. Therefore, if you make a comparison between building in the UK and building in the Netherlands you would have very different opinions of people concerning the design of their bathrooms.

When you design for dementia, familiarity is an important aspect. For instance, having carpet in your bathroom might be very familiar for a British person but it is definitely not for a Dutch person. That is why sometimes it is really important to stick to tradition in building, national tradition, because it adds to the familiarity for people living with dementia.

This makes it very difficult to learn from other countries, because one would always have to make a translation to their national building practices. Too often people who are not very critical do not make this translation. They just copy and paste existing solutions from other countries and try to implement them in their own national context and it does not work.

References

Kort, H. S. M. and van Hoof, J. (2014). Design of a website for home modifications for older persons with dementia. *Technology and Disability* 26 (1): 1–10. doi: 10.3233/TAD-140399.

van Hoof, J., Blom, M. M., Post, H. N. A. and Bastein, W. L. (2013). Designing a "Think-Along Dwelling" for people with dementia: a co-creation project between health care and the building services sector. *Journal of Housing for the Elderly*, 27 (3): 299–332.

Case study 7

Name: Designing interactive music systems with and for people living with dementia

Lead: Alexander Müller-Rakow

Design team: Rahel Flechtner, Nicole Gütl, Juan Pablo Garcia Sossa

Theme: Reminiscence and personhood

Approach/method: User-centred/participatory design/human-centred interaction design

Location: University of the Arts Berlin, Design Research Lab

Case study sources

Articles

Müller-Rakow, A. and Flechtner, R. (2017). Designing interactive music systems with and for people with dementia. *The Design Journal*, 20 (sup1): S2207–S2214.

Website

www.researchgate.net/profile/Alexander_Mueller-Rakow2

Other

Skype interview with Professor Alexander Müller-Rakow

Case study details

Building on the well-established relationship between memory and music, this case study describes an innovative project that both designed and developed an interactive and networked music system for people living with dementia. Three key questions were explored: i) how to design access to digital music platforms; ii) how to take personal biographies and preferences into account when the person's autobiographical memory may be impaired; and iii) how to structure an interactive system that adapts to the cognitive and physical abilities of people living with dementia.

These questions led to the design of an interface of a musical system for use by people living with dementia and its interactive function, namely a personalised photo album that linked autobiographical events to meaningful songs. Interface design was also explored.

Interviews and workshops were used in the development of the design prototype for the musical system, including the use of magnetic cardboard and paper prototypes. Playfulness was reported as a positive and important component of the co-design process. The study reached out to include people with all stages of the lived experience of dementia.

Research method

The co-design team used a participatory and inter-agency approach to addressing the research questions (see: Müller-Rakow and Flechtner, 2017). Relationships were built with people living with dementia and the 'academic'/ design contribution included contributions from the fields of software engineering, hardware engineering, health professionals and retirement home organisations. The research team also considered elements of data privacy and design in the conduct of their work.

In developing the method of study, the design researchers were keen to emphasise the importance of empowering people living with dementia to interact with the developed musical interface so that a radio, for the want of a better description, looked like a radio that people living with dementia could identify with and recognise. Consequently, different design prototypes were arrived at. As an illustration, for some people living with dementia taking part in the study, a radio might look like a piece of separate vintage 'hi-fi' equipment from the 1960s or 1970s where the device is rectangular and has a haptic interface, namely push buttons and rotary knobs. In the UK, for example, the 'hi-fi' manufacturer 'Cambridge Audio' have for many years produced tuners that have an uncluttered facial design and have been popular in the marketplace and speaks to the research team's co-design ambition and the importance of participatory research to gain that insider perspective (see: www.cambridgeaudio.com/gbr/en/about-us/our-history; accessed 24 July 2020).

However, an important design feature was the familiarity of the musical interface to people living with dementia, thus increasing the opportunity for engagement. The wider design research team placed a digital infrastructure into the designed musical interface so that people living with dementia could then confidently identify and interact with the device, but such embedded digital technology would be invisible to person living with dementia as the end user.

The designed musical interface was then linked to a personalised playlist accessed through a photograph album that stored pictures of key memories/

moments of the person living with dementia's life story. The photograph album could then be filled with individual photographs and songs by relatives or care providers with songs that were played back through the musical interface/radio. This was achieved by touching a sensor area on each page of the photograph album. The sensor on each page of the photograph album had a well-known 'play' symbol so that it could be pressed by the person living with dementia resulting in the music system producing music. This association between meaningful and biographical music, a picture representing a moment in time of the person living with dementia's life story, and the music being played from an interactive device that the person living with dementia would recognise as a 'radio', captured the essence of the project. It was of significant importance to the design team that the electronic interfaces were recognised by people living with dementia and accessed via easy-to-handle technology.

A third part of the design method was to explore handling the musical interfaces. The research team purposively avoided any reference to historic devices, symbolic markings and forms in this phase of the study. Instead, emphasis was placed upon generating a new relationship between tangible representations of songs and playlists with soft textiles. Development of this approach called for a need for haptic investigation by people living with dementia as the direct users of the design technology. Consequently, the team trusted in the natural curiosity and creativity of people living with dementia for haptic and physical qualities layered with a need to understand how the interplay of flexible and modular elements stimulated an interactive response. This was achieved by the research team noting the type of playful interfaces that were generated from the workshop observations where textile and soft materials were given to the participants living with dementia.

Whilst these materials were initially intended for the use in mapping methods in the original study design, the research team noted that people living with dementia started to spontaneously 'play' with the given samples. As the researchers noted at the time, the person living with dementia's actions of bouncing, squeezing, sorting and stroking the materials revealed a strong interest in the material quality and structure of soft materials. This led the research team to conclude that playfulness could be a promising approach in the development of design interfaces for people living with dementia, especially in the sharing of soft material combinations to increase the motivation to play.

Lessons learnt

Through the different values and experiences of undertaking the shared design, the research team were aiming to stimulate debate on referential interfaces for people living with dementia and the levels of playfulness that were necessary in order to provide access to digital contents, especially with a focus on music. How these types of interfaces are being deployed in everyday use still needs to be tested, but there is significant potential given the evidence-based attached to music, memories and well-being. Indeed, the literature reveals that there has been a wide range of music programmes used with people living with dementia which range from music therapy delivered by a qualified music therapist to personalised playlists (see: McDermott et al., 2018). Such programmes have been shown to strengthen relationships and to enable people living with dementia to learn new skills (van der Steen et al., 2018). Moreover, there is an emerging literature base from the qualitative literature that reports on how music can help to create meaningful connections between the person living with dementia and others, including care staff, and to strengthen a person's sense of self-identity (Dowlen et al., 2018). This design study adds to this literature, especially the findings of the qualitative literature on music.

Importantly, the study helped the research team to affirm with the wider design field that people living with dementia can be actively involved throughout all stages of the research and development process. This was always an ambition and value of Alexander Müller-Rakow who, during the interview, shared *'people living with dementia were included in the process, even before we started'* and also finding out *'how music is involved in everyday life'*. This would suggest that in order to undertake person-centred design research alongside people living with dementia, all individuals that comprise the research team need to act as one and be genuinely interested in simply getting to know people. As Kitwood (1997) stated some years ago, such connections are built on person-to-person work and open communication. This is important as the participatory research agenda is still in a process of development, especially for people living with the more advanced stages of dementia where access to sensory stimulation and embodied actions are crucial, and this need for further understanding perhaps helps to explain why the sensory stimulation was reported in this study as being such a successful approach.

Throughout the study, the participatory and engagement opportunities, especially framed around playfulness, also helped the research team to derive design guidelines for future projects. As Alexander Müller-Rakow shared, through play the design researchers got to know the *'structure of the person's day'* and found that soft materials were very helpful in this process. Therefore, developing a physical object as an interface rather than a 'right or wrong' approach – such as a 'button' that needed to pressed – was also seen to be important especially when examples were shared when objects could also form a playlist. One of the most important aspects was to adapt the interface to the needs of people living with dementia.

References

Dowlen, R., Keady, J., Milligan, C., Swarbrick, C., Ponsillo, N., Geddes, L. and Riley, B. (2018). The personal benefits of musicking for people living with dementia: a thematic synthesis of the qualitative literature. *Arts & Health*, 10 (3): 197–212.

Kitwood, T. (1997). *Dementia Reconsidered: The Person Comes First*. Buckinghamshire: Open University Press.

McDermott, O., Ridder, H.M., Baker, F.A., Wosch, T., Ray, K. and Stige, B. (2018). Indirect music therapy practice and skill-sharing in dementia care. *Journal of Music Therapy*, 55 (3): 255–279.

Müller-Rakow, A. and Flechtner, R. (2017). Designing interactive music systems with and for people with dementia. *The Design Journal*, 20 (sup1): S2207–S2214.

van der Steen, J., van Soest-Poortvliet, M., van der Wouden, J., Bruinsma, M., Scholten, R. and Vink, A. (2018). *Music-Based Therapeutic Interventions for People with Dementia*. Cochrane Database of Systematic Reviews. 23 July 2018; 7 (7): CD003477. doi: 10.1002/14651858.CD003477.pub4.

Case study 8

Name: The LAUGH project

Lead: Cathy Treadaway

Theme: Design and Methods Innovation

Approach/method: User-centred/compassionate design

Location: Cardiff, Wales (CARIAD, Cardiff Metropolitan University), with international collaborators at the University of Technology Sydney and Coventry University.

Case study sources

Articles

Websites

www.laughproject.info/
www.laughproject.info/home-2/laugh/about-laugh/
www.laughproject.info/wp-content/uploads/2018/04/Compassionate-Design_toolkit.pdf

Other

Skype interview with Professor Cathy Treadaway

Case study details

The LAUGH (Ludic Artefacts Using Gesture and Haptics) research project is a trail-blazing and highly influential study that worked alongside people living with late-stage dementia in order to design innovative playful products whose function was to 'amuse, comfort, engage, bring joy and promote "in the moment" living'. The research team investigated innovative design solutions that incorporated embedded electronics and smart materials.

The LAUGH research project was underpinned by 'Compassionate Design', a new methodological approach created by Cathy Treadaway that aspires to identify the key components when designing for people living with late-stage dementia (Treadaway, 2018). The key components of Compassionate Design are: design that stimulates the senses; that is highly personalised; and that helps to foster connections between people and the world. The approach places loving-kindness at the heart of the design process. The theory is underpinned by positive psychology.

The LAUGH research project provided an opportunity to test the effectiveness of the Compassionate Design approach in practice. This led to the development of six playful object prototypes designed for people living with late-stage dementia. These object prototypes were:

1. HUG by LAUGH™ is a sensory device designed to bring pleasure and comfort to people living with late-stage dementia. HUG by LAUGH™ is designed to be cuddled and the device has a beating heart within a soft body – the sensory object can also play music which can also accommodate a favourite playlist. HUG by LAUGH™ was initially designed for a person who was approaching the end of their life and where verbal communication was significantly compromised. HUG by LAUGH™ connects directly to nurturing and to meet an innate human need to give care to other living things as well as to care for oneself.
2. Giggle balls are soft felt woollen balls that contain electronics such as a small tilt sensor, speakers and microcontroller with sound files of children's laughter. When turned over, the hand the balls 'giggle'.
3. A steering wheel with interactive functioning. This was specifically designed to rekindle the pleasurable act of driving and utilises a microcontroller to provide haptic vibration to simulate the car engine running. The design also has functioning indicators with dashboard lights and a 'tune in' vintage radio that enables a playlist to be accessed of the user's favourite songs.
4. A retro telephone housed in a wooden box. When switched on, the telephone rings spontaneously and adopts a traditional dialling tone sound. The device also plays a random music track from a pre-programmed favourite playlist.
5. Fidget jewellery in a wooden box. Here, three sensory items of jewellery have been designed to rest gently over the fingers and to dangle into the palm of one hand. There are no embedded electronics included in this design and the person living with late-stage dementia can manipulate the fidget jewellery with the fingers of their other hand.
6. Luma is an interactive, hand-held crafted wooden object that was designed to bring a sense of 'the outside' inside.

The LAUGH research project has a dedicated website and received three-year funding from the Arts and Humanities Research Council in the UK. The research project has received interest from a wide-range of influential parties, including the BBC (see: www.bbc.co.uk/news/uk-wales-50237366; accessed 4 August 2020).

Research method

The research team was international in composition although the design and prototype work took place in south Wales. The design research team was partnered by 'Pobl [1] Gwalia Care & Support' (www.poblgroup.co.uk/care-and-support/), one of the largest providers of residential social care in Wales, and brought together people living with dementia, their carers and a range of health professionals, technologists and designers. The work was also supported by leading charities in the field such as Age Cymru, My Home Life Cymru, Alzheimer's Society and Dementia Positive.

The LAUGH research team worked closely with six people living with late-stage dementia in two of the partner organisation's care homes. University ethics approval was obtained to undertake the study and the partner company's protocols were followed to ensure that ongoing, iterative process consent was followed. In terms of method development, the key phases of the LAUGH study were: (i) knowledge gathering via case study and participatory workshops; (ii) reflection via analysis of data from the first phase and development of 'portrait' information; (iii) design scoping and ideation via participatory co-design workshops to inform design and prototyping phase; and (iv) testing and evaluating in an iterative cycle to refine concepts via participatory evaluation workshops. The study also employed 'Live Lab' evaluations with carers to ensure that the emergent designs were safe and that people living with late-stage dementia and their carers were central to the design process.

It is important to highlight that in the first phase of the research, based around 'knowledge gathering', that the research team aimed to understand issues around playfulness, memory and hand-use in relation to dementia. Data analysis of this initial phase of the study led to the identification of six themes that were considered by participants to be widely applicable for people living with late-stage dementia and had the potential for guiding design concept development. These themes were: (i) nurturing, (ii) attention, (iii) movement, (iv) re-play, (v) security and (vi) purposeful. These themes were later related to each of the six design objects that arose from the LAUGH study, further enhancing the validity and authenticity of this analysis.

The team drew on the work of positive design (Desmet and Pohlmeyer, 2013) which identifies pleasure, personal significance and virtue as key components for designing for happiness. This is important as work in late-stage dementia is often overlooked as a focus for research attention (in any field) and lacks an evidence-base that is often developed and promoted in the earlier stages of dementia (see: National Institute for Health and Care Excellence, 2018). As people living with late-stage dementia will lack capacity to consent, this makes the process of involvement a more challenging activity, as noted by the research team (Teadaway et al., 2019). However, overcoming such obstacles is vital if important work, as exemplified by the LAUGH research project, is to be undertaken. The methods and theoretical underpinnings also shifted the narrative in late-stage dementia from one of being a complex and challenging area where little could be achieved, to one which instilled a sense of fun, hope and enjoyment in lived experience. Indeed, the adoption of 'LAUGH' as the title and focal point of the research project, and the operationalisation of 'Compassionate Design', are obvious examples of this narrative turn.

It was noticeable in the overarching research article that explained the processes and design prototypes in the LAUGH project (Treadaway et al., 2019), that observation and case study was such an important feature of the work and in the emergence of the six design protypes. For example, in that article, each of the design prototypes were reported as being developed from a specific 'case' (i.e. lived human experience) where a need was observed in real-time and with a real person living with late-stage dementia, and a design solution offered. That the design solution then went on to have wider appeal and resonance with others is a testament to the design research methods and the vision and values of the whole research team, including all partners involved in the process. As Cathy Treadaway shared during the interview, '*if its right for people with dementia, its probably right for everybody*'.

Lessons learnt

As Treadaway et al. (2019) acknowledged, the LAUGH research project built upon well-being research that demonstrated that happy people live longer, have fewer falls and require less medication. Tellingly, the authors also reveal that 'those who have the greatest need for excellent design are often the most vulnerable in society'. For people living with late-stage dementia, whether in residential care or at home, that statement speaks such truth. In connecting to people living with late-stage dementia, one of the most important lessons learnt from the LAUGH research project was in finding ways to understand the moment-by-moment and everyday experiences. The six design prototypes that evolved from this three-year study all stemmed from this in-the-moment frame of reference.

A few years ago, a major study reviewing the literature on life story work in dementia identified the inability of current measures to capture 'in the moment' benefits and recommended that future studies develop innovative methods to address this research and practice deficit (Gridley et al., 2016). Two years later, a Cochrane Review examining reminiscence and related therapies in dementia care by Woods et al. (2018) reached a broadly similar conclusion and suggested that future psychosocial studies needed to place an 'in the moment' lens against the evaluation of the lived experience. Through Compassionate Design, the LAUGH research project has started to answer these set challenges. Perhaps a significant lesson learnt from undertaking the study is that good research takes time, resources and collaboration and that the project outcomes and social/practice impact continue beyond a funding timeline.

Participatory and emancipatory co-design research needs to be underpinned by empathic and compassionate approaches that places the person (in this case, the person living with late-stage dementia) at the heart of the design process. Compassionate Design was instrumental in reaching the project and design goals. By positioning people living with dementia as key to the co-design process, outcomes can then be produced that significantly benefit the user as well as other stakeholders, such as carers and care providers. In meeting that aspiration, and many others, the LAUGH research project has been, and remains, inspirational.

Note

1 Pobl is Welsh for 'people'.

References

Desmet, P. M. A, and Pohlmeyer, A. E. (2013). Positive design: an introduction to design for subjective wellbeing. *International Journal of Design*, 7(3): 5–19.

Gridley, K., Brooks, J., Birks, Y., Baxter, K. and Parker, G. (2016). *Improving Care for People with Dementia: Development and Initial Feasibility Study for Evaluation of Life Story Work in Dementia Care.* Available at: www.ncbi.nlm.nih.gov/books/NBK379598/

National Institute for Health and Care Excellence. (2018). *Dementia: Assessment, Management and Support for People Living with Dementia and their Carers.* NICE guideline. Published June 2018. Available at: www.nice.org.uk/guidance/ng97

Treadaway, C., Fennell, J., Taylor, A. and Kenning, G. (2019). Designing for playfulness through compassion: design for advanced dementia. *Design for Health*, doi: 10.1080/24735132.2019.1593295.

Woods, B., O'Philbin, L., Farrell, E. M., Spector, A. E. and Orrell, M. (2018). *Reminiscence Therapy for Dementia* (Review). Cochrane Library Cochrane Database of Systematic Reviews. Available at: www.cochranelibrary.com/cdsr/doi/10.1002/14651858.CD001120.pub3/epdf/full

Case study 9

Name: Paul's Club (community resource for younger people living with dementia)

Lead: Alison Phinney

Theme: Design Innovation

Approach/method: Observation and ethnographic approaches

Location: Paul's Club, Vancouver, Canada

Case Study sources

Articles

Kelson, E., Phinney, A., Lowry, G. and Cox, S. (2017). Social citizenship, public art and dementia: walking the urban waterfront with Paul's Club. *Cogent Arts & Humanities*, 4 (1). ISSN 2331-1983 Available at http://openresearch.ocadu.ca/id/eprint/2223/

Phinney, A., Kelson, E., Baumbusch, J., O'Connor, D. and Purves, D. (2016). Walking in the neighbourhood: performing social citizenship in dementia. *Dementia: The International Journal of Social Research and Practice*, 15 (3): 381–394. https://doi.org/10.1177/1471301216638180

Website

https://paulsclub.weebly.com/

Other

Skype interview with Professor Alison Phinney

Case study details

Paul's Club is a social and recreational day programme for people living with young onset dementia (i.e. dementia occurring before the age of 65 years).

Paul's Club opened in 2012 and it is situated in a hotel in downtown Vancouver and meets three times a week. It is the only Club of its type in Vancouver. A maximum of 15 members are able to attend Paul's Club each day and events/activities last for around six hours a day (between 10 am and 4 pm). As part of a daily routine, each day after lunch, the Club members will usually leave their downtown hotel base and take a long walk. A favourite walk is reported as the 'seawall', which is a walking path that follows the shoreline of False Creek, a shallow harbour in the middle of Vancouver that provides recreational opportunities in an area of high-rise residential towers. Club members also interacted with public art when out and about (Kelson et al., 2017).

Paul's Club is not a formal part of either the health or social care systems in Vancouver, although referrals to the Club are often made from one of these sources. The Club is supported through membership fees (set on a sliding scale) with additional funding coming through a variety of fundraising efforts, and more recently, from the regional health authority. Paul's Club has a programme director to maintain a sense of continuity in its activities and has an ethos of 'having fun together', a philosophy that includes the time spent by Club members when they are out and about in Vancouver and in the neighbourhood(s) close to the physical location of the meeting place. Most members of Paul's Club live at home with their spouse (and sometimes with other family members), although there are a few attendees who live alone at home with the support of a care partner or, in limited cases, attend from a local residential care facility. Family members are recorded as 'rarely' attending Paul's Club and that members live with different 'stages' of dementia.

The main focus of this case study is to explore how community-based activity supports the social citizenship of younger people living with dementia whilst accessing outside spaces. A mix of participation observation, interviews, focus groups and documentary analysis methods were used. The research team were well-versed to undertaking this study as both Alison Phinney and Deborah O'Connor were co-directors of the Centre for Research on Personhood in Dementia at the University of British Columbia in Vancouver, and Professor O'Connor was one of the originators of social citizenship in dementia (see for example: Bartlett and O'Connor, 2007, 2010).

Research method

The reported evaluation of Paul's Club was a sub-set of a larger evaluation study undertaken by the research team. However, in all their work, the research team were keen to explore the benefits of community groups for people living with dementia and the research design had two key objectives. Firstly, to explore how community-based programming can promote social citizenship for people living with dementia. Secondly, to evaluate qualitative methods for including people living with dementia in the research process. University ethical approval was obtained prior to undertaking the study.

During the two-year project, the research team primarily undertook participant observation of Paul's Club members and their everyday activities to arrive at the study findings. Participant observations were turned into fieldnotes and these were supplemented by photographs taken by Club leaders during meetings and when out and about for walks and other excursions in the neighbourhood. These photographs were also turned into a slideshow by the research team so that Club members could reflect and discuss the contents and locations of the material, a process that also formed part of the overall data analysis. The research team also undertook a focus group with Club members and leaders, interviews with family carers and documentary analysis of the Clubs' website and promotional literature.

Through 58 sessions with Paul's Club, the research team generated over 400 hours of participant observation and the primary positioning of the researcher was one of a 'friend of Paul's Club', thus enabling an insider view to everyday activities. As stated by Phinney et al. (2016), the focus of the participatory observations was on members' actions and interactions within the physical and social environment, as well as the verbal and non-verbal exchanges within the group. Notes were written during each session, sometimes captured through the text function on a smartphone, to document what was happening, especially the verbatim comments from Club members. These materials were subsequently developed into more detailed ethnographic, reflexive field notes. Data was analysed interpretively using the general inductive approach and specific attention was placed on exploring how aspects of social citizenship were constructed and revealed through the group's practice of walking in the city.

One of the method insights that developed from the research was that the walking interviews allowed for spontaneous conversations between Club members in an unstructured form. Such interaction allowed the research team to capture conversations in short narratives which were referred to as 'walking vignettes'. One of the interesting dimensions of such walking vignettes was that the everyday natural environment, such as the weather, became prompts for conversations between members and the landscape held memories for members that could also be shared. Thus, walking was an embodied and sensory experience that connected the person to natural world. Such connections were vitally important, as captured in the following quote which is included on the Paul's Club website:

> *I think what has been so important for John (who is 58) is that going to Paul's Club has brought him out of his shell and I think he feels more 'normal' and is much happier. I would think his participation has even slowed down this devastating disease. I cannot return to work as I would need before and after club care and also care on the other days of the week.*

Interpretive analysis of the data revealed how aspects of social citizenship were constructed and revealed through the Club's everyday practice of walking in the city, framed as a neighbourhood. Three major themes emerged: i) Keeping the focus off dementia, which was about continuing with everyday activities, such as walking, using humour to 'keep things light' and enjoying being in the company of other Club members; ii) Creating a place of belonging, which was about the Club leaders, Club members, friends, and families being clear that everyone is able to share in an activity that is meaningful and enjoyable. This was seen during the walks when Club members were shifting conversational groups and being in the company of other Club members; and iii) Claiming a place in the community, which was about Club members continuing to have an identity as citizens and continuing to do small things, such as stopping to engage with and play with dogs when out and about for a walk, chatting with the owners and so on. Significantly, for Paul's Club members to be out and about and visible to others in the neighbourhood and downtown Vancouver, was, in its own way, a means of combatting prejudice and stigma that is often associated with living with dementia. To be visible and to own the identity of a younger person living with dementia is an important personal statement, and journey.

Lessons learnt

The lessons learnt in this case study need to be placed within a definition of social citizenship which Bartlett and O'Connor (2010) saw as 'a relationship, practice or status in which the person living with dementia is entitled to experience freedom from discrimination, and to have opportunities to grow and participate in life to the fullest extent possible' (p. 37). As Alison Phinney shared during the interview, in the early days of creating the ethos behind Paul's Club with those interested in setting it up, Alison's advice was *'to foster social connection and to have fun'* and that *'people have their own solutions'*.

One of the lessons learnt from the research study was that social citizenship is flexible when enacted. As Phinney et al. (2016) state 'explaining how the group's practice of walking through the neighbourhood constructs social citizenship in terms of positioning, participation and community may contribute to further theorizing, but hopefully has practical implications as well' (p. 391). This is important as in designing for dementia there is a need to move beyond the technical and see the practical and the mundane in everyday life and in empowering citizens to take control of their own lives. Such emancipatory and participatory approaches are not simple and investment in different relationships is necessary to help support younger people living with dementia to enhance their everyday life and well-being. Finding meaning in such activities and situations would appear an important value-base to take forward.

Indeed, theoretical insights into everyday life are often framed around notions of atmosphere, belonging and time, areas which readily intersect with people living with dementia (of all ages). One area that design researchers might take away from this study is the value of including the mundane and the everyday in methods development, and that the natural world helps to connect people living with dementia to people, spaces and places.

Recently, Lesley Calvert, a younger person living with dementia in the UK, has developed ideas around 'place-attachment disruption' which is about familiar parts of the neighbourhood becoming unfamiliar to people living with dementia and the anxiety caused by such an accumulating event, which may well result in people living with dementia staying in instead of going out (Calvert et al., 2020). How familiarity and friendships formed in Paul's Club helps to mitigate against these circumstances could form a new direction for research attention, combined with the creative social research methods shared in case study.

References

Bartlett, R. and O'Connor, D. (2007). From personhood to citizenship: broadening the lens for dementia practice and research. *Journal of Aging Studies*, 21 (2): 107–118.

Bartlett, R. and O'Connor, D. (2010). *Broadening the Dementia Debate, Towards Social Citizenship*. Bristol: The Policy Press.

Calvert, L., Keady, J., Khetani, B., Riley, C., Open Doors Research Group and Swarbrick, C. (2020). '… this is my home and my neighbourhood with my very good and not so good memories': The story of autobiographical place-making and a recent life with dementia. *Dementia: The International Journal of Social Research and Practice*, 19 (1): 111–128.

Kelson, E., Phinney, A., Lowry, G. and Cox, S. (2017). Social citizenship, public art and dementia: Walking the urban waterfront with Paul's Club. *Cogent Arts & Humanities*, 4 (1). ISSN 2331-1983 Available at http://openresearch.ocadu.ca/id/eprint/2223/

Phinney, A., Kelson, E., Baumbusch, J., O'Connor, D. and Purves, D. (2016). Walking in the neighbourhood: Performing social citizenship in dementia. *Dementia: The International Journal of Social Research and Practice*, 15 (3): 381–394

Case study 10

Name: The 'in the moment' musical experiences of people living with dementia
Lead: Robyn Dowlen
Theme: Improvised music-making
Approach/method: Multiple-case study
Location: Greater Manchester, UK

Case study sources

Articles/academic outputs

Website

www.cameratacommunity.co.uk/dementia/

Other

Face-to-face interview with Robyn Dowlen

Case study details

This case study explores the use of setting up and undertaking case study research with people living with dementia attending a series of improvised music-making sessions. The case study showcases the work of 'Music in Mind' (as part of the work of Manchester Camerata) and explored processes and procedures involved in capturing and recording the 'in the moment' experiences of all involved in the music-making space. This became the overarching research question.

The work formed the basis of a three-year full-time PhD study conducted by Robyn Dowlen (Dowlen, 2018) which was funded by an ESRC CASE studentship. The Universities of Manchester and Lancaster were the academic partners and Manchester Camerata the CASE partner. Robyn positioned herself as a participant-observer within one 15-week community-based Music in Mind programme and used various creative research methods to document and report upon the activities that were undertaken. The principles of Music in Mind are centred on choice and agency for the person living with dementia and the programme enables a democratisation of the music space through supported improvisation using percussive instruments, the human voice and body percussion

The methods used during the three-year study included participant observation, video-based observation, video-elicitation interviews and participant diaries. The groups' activities in the Music in Mind sessions were video recorded via digital cameras from weeks 5 to week 15 and formed a significant part of the data analysis procedure and practices.

People living with dementia who took part in the study mainly lacked capacity to consent and therefore seeking appropriate ethical consent procedures through the Social Care Research Ethics Committee in the UK was necessary (ref: 16/IEC08/0049). Family carers also formed part of the Music in Mind groups alongside people living with dementia as well as the Music in Mind musicians and music therapist.

Research method

As the creative research methods were conducted through Music in Mind sessions, it is important to consider the main tenets of this approach and how each session is run. Established in 2012, Manchester Camerata's Music in Mind is a music therapy-based programme for people living with dementia and their care partners. Music in Mind is co-facilitated by a music therapist and a Manchester Camerata orchestral musician. The principles of Music in Mind are centred on choice and agency for the person living with dementia, enabling a democratisation of the musical space through supported improvisation using percussion instruments, the human voice and body percussion.

Each Music in Mind programme is delivered over a period of 10–20 weeks and each session follows the same structure. The room, or space within a room, which is intended for the programme, is set up so that a circle of chairs is placed around a central table which contains an array of percussion instruments. Music in Mind practitioners position themselves within the circle of chairs rather than in a position that would suggest it is a musical performance which separates 'audience' and 'performer'. This is a non-verbal indication of a collaborative music-making approach, with every contribution in the circle viewed as valid and each person viewed as a musician rather than separated by role or diagnosis.

The practitioners typically start the sessions with a 'Welcome Song'. This song is consistent across the duration of the programme to allow for a non-verbal signal that the music-making is beginning and to acknowledge each group member's presence. The 'Welcome Song' is followed by the creative music-making part of the session, which provides an extended time usually lasting between 30 and 60 minutes for people living with dementia to explore the different percussion instruments on offer to them, creating new music through supported improvisation, musical games, as well as singing and improvising around familiar music. Sessions are ended by the practitioners through a 'Goodbye Song', which is again consistent across the duration of the programme.

By being a participant observer to one community-based Music in Mind programme, Robyn was able to recruit six people living with dementia into the study, four family carers and two practitioners who were delivering the Music in Mind sessions, a music therapist and a Manchester Camerata musician. At the time of recruitment, the mean age of group members who were living with dementia was 62, with all but one living with a diagnosis of a young onset dementia. The main research methods consisted of:

1. Video-based observation via recoding the sessions using three video cameras. In order to build the relationship between Robyn and each participant, and to ensure each group member had provided consent/personal consultee agreement, the cameras were not turned on until week 5 of the programme. Two cameras were place on tripods within the music-making circle and the third was operated by the researcher from within the circle in order to capture close-ups of individual music-making events.
2. Video-elicitation interviews via Robyn identifying video clips each of around 5–10 minutes in length from the video recording of the Music in Mind sessions to show to participants as part of video-elicitation interviews. These interviews lasted between 60 and 120 minutes and took place within participants' homes and gave an opportunity to 're-live' the sessions outside of the context of the physical music-making space. The practitioners were interviewed together in a neutral space and they brought their research diaries to the interviews and requested video clips they wanted to review ahead of the interview.
3. Participant diaries used by family carers and practitioners as a means of reflecting on the programme outside of the session time or video-elicitation interviews. Diaries were guided by three broad questions: i) What happened during the Music in Mind session?; ii) What are your reflections on what happened during the session? iii) Are there any moments that were particularly poignant to you, and if so, why?

From analysis of the overall data set, three themes were developed that captured 'in the moment' musical experience: i) sharing a life story through music; ii) being 'in the moment' with music; and iii) musical ripples into everyday life (Dowlen, 2018; Dowlen, accepted for publication). These themes highlight the creativity and musical abilities of people living with dementia whilst showcasing music as a medium to connect people living with dementia with their own life story, other people and the environments in which music-making takes place.

Lessons learnt

In the dementia field, the creativity of people living with dementia has rarely been captured and one of the main lessons from this research study was that this focus is possible, but a new approach and values-base is needed that *wants* to capture such lived experiences. In the PhD study (Dowlen, 2018), the importance of developing 'in the moment profiles'(IMPs) was put forward as such a new approach to recording the processes and outcomes of the creative process. Directly linked to this point, there is growing body of work in the dementia studies literature that supports the importance of 'little-c', or everyday creativity, being showcased by people living with dementia (Bellass et al., 2018). This everyday creativity was seen in and across the findings of the study with people living with dementia showing improvisatory creativity both in the music they improvised and the ways in which they used their embodied practices to construct musical stories through gesture and facial expression (Dowlen et al., accepted for publication). For design researchers, using video and creative methods that start to document the sensory and embodied experiences of people living with dementia could be an important future direction, especially when underpinned by a participatory research approach that allows situations to be relived once again.

Engagement with music also helps to combat feelings of social isolation and stigma for people living with dementia and their family carers (where such a relationship exists) and it provides an opportunity to create connections through 'in the moment' musical interaction. This is important as musical interaction is not reliant on verbal communication or cognitive capacities and sound and rhythm can carry significant embodied emotion. As Robyn stated during the interview, her research took a more applied look at embodied research so that *'it's not just about reporting on these embodied and sensory experiences but actually saying, okay, this is where the person is, how might we use this to understand and measure better within this area'*.

The study also highlighted the value of 'moments' in dementia care. Interestingly, exploring what is a 'moment' and their significance is an underresearched area in the literature, despite the need that 'moments' constitute an important frame of reference in better understanding the lived experience of dementia (Woods et al., 2018). Using design research principles to explore the meaning and response to 'moments' may prove a fruitful and innovative future direction.

References

Bellass, S., Balmer, A., May, V., Keady, J., Buse, C., Capstick, A., Burke, L., Bartlett, R. and Hodgson, J. (2018). Broadening the debate on creativity and dementia: a critical approach. *Dementia: The International Journal of Social Research and Practice*, Advance online publication. Retrieved from https://doi.org/10.1177/1471301218760906

Dowlen, R. (2018). *The 'in the moment' musical experiences of people with dementia: a multiple case study approach.* PhD thesis. The University of Manchester, Manchester, UK.

Dowlen, R., Keady, J., Milligan, C., Swarbrick, C., Ponsillo, N., Geddes, L. and Riley, B. (accepted for publication). In the moment with music: an exploration of the embodied and sensory experiences of people living with dementia during improvised music-making. Submitted to *Ageing & Society*, June 2020 and accepted February, 2021.

Dowlen, R., Keady, J., Milligan, C., Swarbrick, C., Ponsillo, N., Geddes, L. and Riley, B. (2018). The personal benefits of musicking for people living with dementia: a thematic synthesis of the qualitative literature. *Arts and Health: An International Journal*, 10(3): 197–212.

Woods, B., O'Philbin, L., Farrell, E. M., Spector, A. E. and Orrell, M. (2018). *Reminiscence Therapy for Dementia* (Review). Cochrane Library Cochrane Database of Systematic Reviews. Available at: www.cochranelibrary.com/cdsr/doi/10.1002/14651858.CD001120.pub3/epdf/full

Part 3
Foresight

6 The future
Current challenges and emerging opportunities

Introduction

The chapters and case studies presented in the book, thus far, have presented a picture of the state-of-the-art in design research, including the current challenges in the design field. In several chapters we have also provided insights and awareness about how, and where, design research can make a significant contribution to the field. In doing so, we have identified research practices and new areas of research that need to change and progress in order to fully address the challenges people living with dementia, their caregivers and society as a whole face.

In this final chapter we want to move a step further and explore beyond the state-of-the-art research. We will do this by offering a foresight into design research and identifying how some of the key challenges in the field of dementia can be transformed into opportunities for future design research. We will also highlight several emerging trends for design researchers which we have identified through three sources. Firstly, the literature reviews that underpinned previous chapters in this book; secondly, by considering the contribution of the ten case studies in Part 2 of the text; and thirdly, by drawing on our own immersion in the dementia studies field over the years and arriving at some previously unspoken thoughts about moving the design research field forward. However, we will start the chapter by considering people living with dementia as co-researchers and imagining how this contribution might play out in times to come.

People living with dementia as co-researchers

Increasing the participation of people with dementia in research is a global priority (Bartlett et al., 2018). Nevertheless, there is very limited research on the experiences of persons living with dementia, with evaluators and researchers having largely failed to fully access the direct experience of people living with dementia (Gray et al., 2017). Until recently, the focus on experiences of dementia has been on medical and cognitive aspects and the impact on carers and their experiences (Johannessen and Möller, 2013). It is, therefore, clear from both the literature and the case studies presented in this book that the voice of people living in dementia needs to be enhanced. This missing voice has so far resulted in the person living with dementia's own perspective, subjective experiences and aspirations being largely absent from research within the field.

Although unintentional, people living with dementia mainly assume a passive role in research, with research 'done to them' as opposed to 'with them'. This is partly due to the predominantly medicalised/clinical focus of dementia research that continues to employ quantitative methods to assess the efficacy and effectiveness of interventions, be that psychosocial or otherwise. However, experiences of living with dementia are difficult to cover with quantitative methods alone and qualitative methods are required in improving knowledge in areas where little is previously known (Johannessen and Möller, 2013; Calvert et al., 2020).

Furthermore, challenges in accessing groups of people living with dementia and involving them in research (as outlined in Chapter 3) whether logistical, or due to current medically-dominated ethical procedures and protocols (Hubbard et al., 2003; McKeown et al., 2010; Gray et al., 2017), lead to caregiver-focused research or research that explores the experience of people living with dementia through their caregivers (Moore and Hollett, 2003; Brodaty and Donkin, 2009; McKeown et al., 2010). This approach of 'research by proxy' is also impacting the development of interventions that materialise the power relationship in care situations, which risk them being used unnecessarily and in ways that may harm the care recipient (Iltanen-Tähkävuori et al., 2012).

Conducting research with people living with dementia as co-researchers and/or designing interventions, services with people living with dementia as co-designers are critical in addressing the aforementioned gaps in the literature and are gradually starting to emerge. More precisely, co-design is defined as collective creativity as it is applied across the whole span of a design process. According to Sanders and Stappers (2008), co-design *'refers to the creativity of designers and people not trained in design working together in the design development process'* (p. 7). Co-design presents a fundamental shift in the traditional designer–user relationship. The co-design approach enables a wide range of people to make a creative contribution in the solution but critically also in the formulation of a problem, a task that has been predominantly led by designers previously. A key element of co-design is that users, such as people living with dementia, as 'domain experts' of their own needs and experiences (Visser et al., 2005), become central to the design process. In this process designer's role shifts from that of a translator (of user experiences/needs) to that of a facilitator (Sanders and Stappers, 2008) providing ways for people to engage with each other as well as providing ways to communicate, be creative, share insights and test out new ideas. Building and deepening equal collaboration between users and designers is a critical aspect of the co-design philosophy (White and Pettit,

2007). Engaging with each other, communicating and sharing insights is an important part of co-design, as it helps to develop an empathic relationship between researchers and research participants, benefitting both people living with dementia but also researchers embarking on this field for the first time. This contributes to an improved understanding of the dementia research domain and the issues that people living with dementia, as experts in their own domain, encounter.

For instance, the Disrupting Dementia tartan project shows how co-design methods and tools can enable people living with dementia to make a significant contribution to society after diagnosis. Specifically, this project has clearly demonstrated that people living with dementia can offer much to society, as through co-design they can contribute to the development of a commercially available mass-produced product. And in doing so, the project has helped reconnect people recently diagnosed with dementia to build their self-esteem, identity and dignity and keep the person living with dementia connected to their local community (Rodgers, 2018). It is therefore clear that people living with dementia can and should be involved in the design and evaluation of services and interventions.

Nevertheless, designing collaboratively with people living with dementia in a co-design process is very challenging (Hendriks et al., 2014). Having looked at several case studies that employed a co-design approach whilst working with people living with dementia, Hendriks et al. (2013) developed 33 guidelines. These aimed as a starting point for researchers and designers who were setting up participatory projects with people living with dementia. A couple of years later, their work, along with workshops held with other researchers active in the field, led them to advocate a highly individual approach towards adjusting co-design techniques (Hendriks et al., 2015). Furthermore, Tsekleves et al. (2020) argue that for people living with dementia, participatory arts activities and co-design are most accessible as collaborative mixes of co-design and co-creation, and that realistically it is not helpful to insist on pure forms of co-design.

Researchers have the social responsibility to do so and design researchers are well placed to enable this through research methods such as co-design. To further facilitate and enable this research institutions and researchers will need to take steps to adapt methods to allow active participation of people living with dementia (McKeown et al., 2010). This is an opportunity for the research community, particularly in areas such as in inclusive design, design for health, design for change and design methods to take a lead in this effort.

Apart from researchers, research institutions and especially ethics committees and procedures required adapting to enable people living with dementia participating more actively in research as co-researchers. It is recommended that future research outlines how individuals living with dementia are included, how they consent, how decisions are made between two approaches to consent when a combination of approaches are used and how they are supported throughout the research process (Daly Lynn et al.,

2019. The challenges related to the current ethical procedures provide opportunities for researchers with interest in ethics and participatory research, who can play a leading role in redefining this.

Design for agency and daily living

The majority of research-to-date places most of the focus on medical and clinical needs with little attention paid on the emotional needs and daily living activities of people living with dementia (Kenning and Treadaway, 2018). Regarding the latter, there is limited research on quality of life of people living with dementia. Therefore, we need more research focusing on the broader 'quality of life' aspects (e.g. the physical environment's effect on positive engagement in an activity, planned or spontaneous), rather than research primarily focusing on environment and challenging behaviours or functional abilities (Chaudhury and Cooke, 2014). These are all areas that design research can address through its creative research approaches, helping the community develop a better understanding of a day in the life of a person with dementia. Design ethnography methods are well suited to help address this by paying more attention not only to the functional but also to the environmental and emotional needs of persons living with dementia.

This shift from research on challenging behaviours and environmental security measures to research on personal identity and daily living activities requires that as researchers we approach dementia from a well-being and quality of life perspective, not one of cognitive decline and disability.

Looking at the home and care environment, the focus will need to shift from safety to comfort. This can be reflected in the design of the environment itself and the design of more socially supportive interventions. In terms of the former, scholars have called for more emphasis on how the physical and social environment can be adapted to support the preservation of continuity and identity for persons living with dementia (Førsund et al., 2018). If we want to improve the physical care environment, all the actors involved should be ready to compromise and be willing to focus on the main aims of the care services, and to clarify the core values in care provision and care practices. It should always be remembered that the utmost priority must be the well-being of the person in care. If efficiency is made the main priority, it is impossible thereafter to guarantee good quality services (Iltanen-Tähkävuori et al., 2012). It is, therefore, clear that future research should also look for elements promoting comfort in addition to safety in order to address all aspects of the home experience for both people living with dementia and their family carers (Soilemezi et al., 2017).

Regarding interventions, they can be redesigned to make it easier for carers to converse and develop and maintain relationships with the person living with dementia, rather than simply keeping the person entertained (Subramaniam and Woods, 2010). This is key, as current practice often places the pressure of stimulating and sustaining conversation upon the caregiver, while the person living with dementia commonly assumes a more passive role (Gowans et al., 2007). To further accomplish person-centred interventions, we need to provide individualised activities that promote feelings of purpose and accomplishment, enabling the person living with dementia to remain active, supporting the maintaining of everyday skills such as self-care (Jakob and Collier, 2017). Carefully designed artefacts can be used to create participation that is meaningful for people living with dementia, and can provide researchers with ways to use this participation to drive forward design (Morrissey et al., 2016). Designed artefacts which are personalised with content that is relevant to the individuals living with dementia and their social circle, will help attend to the uniqueness and personhood of people living with dementia and provide opportunities for meaningful communication, so that social relationships are maintained. In this context, personalising can constitute an opportunity for the person living with dementia to exercise control and choice, through selecting content and co-designing an artefact, and simultaneously allow family members to reflect upon and understand their relative while being involved in a collective activity (Branco et al., 2017).

Attention should be placed when one employs IT solutions to ensure that they are not used as 'babysitting' tools but aim towards agency. The Internet of Things (IoT) creates opportunities that provide both patients and people at home a protagonistic role in the caring and management of their health (Pasluosta et al., 2015; Wang et al., 2017). IoT refers to technologies and research disciplines that enable the Internet to reach out into the real world of physical objects (Xia et al., 2012). These includes everyday household products, such as the kettle, lights, cooking appliances and several more. Thus, provided services are carefully designed with people living with dementia (through co-design) and their caregivers and can provide significant support in terms of independence and daily living. Also, for caregivers and people living with dementia, being able to monitor one's health and wellness, will provide empowerment and more personalised health and care. Opportunities for design research include exploring how to best integrate IoT in the home environment, how to develop peer networks and empower individuals to manage their health more effectively and how to design products and services aimed at person-centred home care and wellness.

Artefacts, which provide sensory experiences can trigger emotional memories – a feeling of pleasure can be created when remembering previously positively experienced emotions (Jakob and Collier, 2017) and have shown promise in engaging and stimulating people living with dementia (Morrissey et al., 2016; Kenning and Treadaway, 2018) – demonstrating that even in the later stages of dementia people can interact meaningfully when prompted specifically (Gowans et al., 2007).

As presented in Case study 3 in this book, artefacts (i.e. products) can intentionally or unintentionally also communicate the users' fragility and how their needs are met in care services, such as in the case of the hygiene overalls. Even if the product is designed to be more dignifying, the design itself cannot solve the ethical dilemma concerning use. That is why guidelines and regulations are needed for the use of such products (Iltanen-Tähkävuori et al., 2012) and product designers need to work closely with service designers, care staff and policy-makers as well.

Evidence-based design/co-design

Study of the design literature in the field of dementia along with interviews with experts has revealed two important aspects regarding the majority of the research to date. Namely, lack of rigour in research, specifically the evaluation of dementia-based interventions, and replication of pilot research studies.

Regarding the former, greater methodological rigour is advocated by those who view the primary aim of research as investigating whether and how design and arts activity might be integrated within evidence-based practice (Gray et al., 2017). Within published design research in dementia, there is often lack of detail and robustness in the methodological approaches employed for the design of interventions but also critically their evaluation. The current literature indicates that, although there has been a focus on the development of dementia-specific measures, and measurement of quality of life, the majority of measurement is undertaken for validation purposes, for example, as an indication of the success/impact of an intervention. Despite growing design research in the field of dementia where higher quality of life is the main outcome measure, there is little evidence that an understanding of higher quality of life for people living with dementia is translating into improved or evidenced-based practice (Moyle and Murfield, 2013).

This is also due to challenges with the current evaluation methodologies employed. The qualitative methodologies design researchers often employed are great in providing a nuanced and in-depth understanding of changes an intervention might have on the personhood, emotional needs or specific aspects of a person's quality of life. However, these need to be used consistently using specific measures across research teams and projects so that it is possible to replicate by others. Study of the literature reveals that there is a vast discrepancy of how the design research community currently evaluates interventions for people living with dementia with lack of robustness and consistency being common. Furthermore, although qualitative research is beneficial within the field of dementia intervention evaluation, it can be strengthened and increase its robustness by integrating quantitative research methods too. On the whole, design research does not fully employ quantitative methods, which in this context would be useful in providing the data that policy-makers, decision-makers and clinicians usually expect and consult in implementing services. Currently, the 'so what does this mean in practice' remains largely unanswered or addressed by the research (Moyle and Murfield, 2013). Undertaking more mixed methods research would only strengthen the qualitative research aspects of design research by providing another layer of data, explaining what this would mean in practice. For example, being able to demonstrate that an intervention has shown to increase several elements in a recognised well-being index/framework, which, at the same time, meant that 'person A' could for the first time after many years connect and communicate with their partner, is far more impactful than simply a number or the personal improvement without the other data.

To increase the rigour and robustness of qualitative methods we should, as a design research community, develop and share validated evaluation frameworks and wherever possible employ evidence-based design. An increasing base of research suggests that evidence-based design can be used in parallel with evidence-based medicine to create healthcare systems and processes that support patient care and safety (Ulrich et al., 2008). Healthcare design is increasingly guided by rigorous research linking hospitals' physical environments to healthcare outcomes (Ulrich et al., 2008; Shoemaker et al., 2010; Van Hoof et al., 2015). Evidence-based design, derived from evidence-based medicine, requires full-bodied research efforts and a large amount of valid information, resulting from systematic reviews of research literature that can be applied in practice (Zimring and Bosch, 2008). It is therefore imperative that we develop a repertoire of strategies that can be used with different individuals participating in research (Hubbard et al., 2003). This forms an opportunity for design researchers to adapt existing design research methods and/or develop new ones.

Another challenge to overcome and where opportunities present themselves, is the current state of design research where, in terms of methodological approach, most of the research is still at a preliminary or pilot study level (Subramaniam and Woods, 2010). On one hand, a lack of longitudinal design research studies limits the impact of the research and the full exploration of design research in this field. On the other hand, there is research replication with several pilot projects running in different regions and countries, demonstrating lack of awareness and sharing of similar research.

The reasons behind this are numerous and relate to structural challenges in the funding of design and humanities research in dementia, limited interaction between design research community in the field of dementia, lack of indexed design research repository of papers/projects in dementia research and several other. It is clear from the above, that there is an opportunity to bring the design research community together in the field of dementia through dedicated conferences, forums, special interest groups and the development of open repository of design research studies that will help avoid replication of research and enable the development of more rigour in our field.

Researcher training on working with people living with dementia

As presented in Chapter 2 (section People) and Chapter 3 (section Contexts) in this book, working in the context of dementia and most importantly with people living with dementia requires that researchers are versed in several different areas. Therefore, an opportunity is presented here for research and training programmes that help develop these skills for early career researchers but also experienced researchers who wish to apply their research within the context of dementia.

Working with people living with dementia, one soon discovers that even those who were initially thought to be less active are in fact communicating and interacting but in very nuanced verbal and non-verbal ways. For people living with dementia, even slightest movement is often something that is highly intentional and meaningful (Morrissey et al., 2016). Thus, building opportunities for gesture and movement into designing for and with people living with dementia has the potential to capture a dimension of communication that goes unnoticed too often. Furthermore, realising that communication is collaborative, and problems in interaction are, hence, co-constructed, enables the design of interventions that support co-managing interactions between people living with dementia and their family members or other caregivers, helping to maintain relations for longer (Jones, 2015).

As such, researchers within the field of dementia should be trained as skilled verbal and non-verbal communicators, and be sensitive to and cognisant of the ways in which dementia impacts on a person's memory, decision-making capacity and emotional disposition (Hubbard et al., 2003). This approach entails design researchers acquiring some knowledge on key theories related to neurology, such as neuroplasticity – the brain's ability to reorganise itself by forming new neural connections throughout life (Vance et al., 2010). What this basically means is that even in the case of people living with dementia, specific activities (parts of the brain) can be reinforced through developing appropriate interventions that encourage these (Herholz et al., 2013). This is important as it will enable researchers to design more effective interventions that take into account these important aspects of our baring physiology and capacity.

Apart from this, such approach requires researchers to familiarise themselves with and apply creativity that relies more on the emotional, sensitive and empathetic interactions of people rather than on their verbal expressiveness (Hubbard et al., 2003). Although creativity and empathy are qualities often associated with design researchers, additional training is required on non-verbal communication.

Another area for further training and development is that of intervention implementation. Typically, research focuses on the development of interventions that will improve the quality of life of people living with dementia. As expected, the emphasis is on the efficacy, effectiveness and acceptance of the interventions. However, the literature shows that often the success of a dementia-based intervention is not only depending on system design, but also on the right usage of the system and its integration in the care process (Murko and Kunze, 2015). Removing implementation barriers in care-home settings and in the built environment require understanding of staff resourcing, financial schemes and service financing (Soilemezi et al., 2017). These are aspects often overlooked in research projects, where persuasive economic evaluation appears elusive, perhaps because of a lack of research designs suitable for robust comparative cost analysis and able to satisfactorily address questions of causality (Gray et al., 2017).

To address these there needs to be a shift in the training of researchers to incorporate economic evaluation methods in their research approaches and work more closely with health economists wherever possible. In order to better appreciate the barriers to intervention implementation in the health and care setting, it is recommended that design researchers engage through their institutions and research councils in programmes of secondments or sabbaticals in such settings, such as care homes.

In addition to this, researchers should work with policymakers and providers to ensure that the innovations that they propose to evaluate are policy relevant, fully implementable in the context of the research evaluation, and capable of being taken to scale in the event that effectiveness and cost-effectiveness are demonstrated (Prince et al., 2016). This is an area where opportunities exists for researchers interested or with expertise in design policy.

Emerging and unexplored research areas

There are several unexplored areas in the field of dementia thus constituting emerging areas that researchers can pursue. Namely conducting research studies in Global South countries, focusing on dementia prevention and dementia and gender.

The literature and case studies in the book reveal that there has been limited research outside the developed world, the Global North (Maestre, 2012; Wortmann et al., 2012; Johnston et al., 2019). This is a paradox, especially if one considers that two thirds of people with dementia live in low- and middle-income countries, including China, which have undeveloped dementia service systems and underreported caregiver challenges (Wang et al., 2014). This clearly forms an opportunity for expanding research and studies into the developing world, the Global South.

The lack of studies in Global South countries is not merely an outcome of research neglect but of several reasons that make conducting studies in these contexts challenging. It is not possible to simply transport a study conducted in a Global North to a Global South country, as the cultural, linguistic, economic and social structures will be so different that will require adapting the research methods and also areas of research focus (Ferri and Jacob, 2017; Johnston et al., 2019). For instance, caregiver practice for people living with dementia in China is socially, culturally and politically constructed, with role of family being central part of the caregiver services (Wang et al., 2014). Also, in conducting a dementia study in India, the focus would be primarily on understanding the stigma associated socially and culturally with it before developing any culturally-appropriate interventions (Semrau et al., 2015; Prince et al., 2008).

Differences in the education systems between Global North-South countries coupled with cultural factors result in different perceptions about abstract thinking. In design research, especially in participatory workshops, abstract thinking is often a useful tool employed in looking at the bigger picture and making sense of different types of information. This challenge extends beyond workshops to other design research methods, as some researchers find it difficult to fully understand and contextualise open-ended questions (Cheema et al., 2018). This, coupled with language barriers and cultural hegemony, results in lack of salience of concepts, the non-equivalence of concepts, and the use of levels of language not easily comprehensible to people with limited education (Casale et al., 2011).

The literature has articulated a set of funding, organisational and paradigmatic constraints on research partnerships with potential negative consequences at institutional and individual levels (Godoy-Ruiz et al., 2016). The issues covered include the selection and training of local personnel, the recruitment of participants, sampling challenges, participants' compensation, survey methods and implementation, elicitation methods, the literacy rate of the population and security/ safety issues in developing countries (Durand-Morat et al., 2015). The most frequently mentioned challenges in conducting research in Global South contexts relate to access to data, data collection issues, diversity of the region, language barriers and lack of research support infrastructure (Lages et al., 2015).

Therefore, although conducting design research in the field of dementia in the Global South introduces a new context where cultural, social, religious as well as administrative practices often pose challenges, it can create new exciting opportunities for researchers and for engaging people living with dementia beyond the Global North.

In the absence of a cure, at the time of writing this book, significant research effort has been focusing on the treatment of the symptoms of people living with dementia. This is an absolutely vital effort in improving the quality of life people currently living with dementia, but focus should be also given into research targeting its prevention. Today, the optimal approach to addressing the impending public health crisis of dementia has been the prevention of onset and progression of the disease. Given that current dementia treatments can only target the symptoms of dementia and do not offer cure or modify the underlying disease process, research focusing on prevention of dementia is essential to mitigate future sufferings and costs (Chen et al., 2014).

There is sufficiently strong research evidence (Mangialasche et al., 2012; Norton et al., 2014; Livingston et al., 2017) for encouraging individuals to reduce their risk of dementia through targeting modifiable risk factors in mid-life. General prevention strategies that are being tested include reducing vascular risk factors, such as hypertension, diabetes, physical inactivity, (midlife) obesity, hyperlipidemia and smoking that are associated with both vascular and Alzheimer's disease type dementia (Chen et al., 2014; Deckers et al., 2015).

Protective factors for dementia and AD have also been identified; these include high education and socioeconomic status in early life as well as a number of factors in adult life: high work complexity, rich social network, social engagement, mentally stimulating activity, nonsmoking and regular physical exercise (Mangialasche et al., 2012; Deckers et al., 2015). Intervention at the correct age for prevention of the aforementioned risk factors could reduce the prevalence of dementia significantly (Norton et al., 2014). This is true, even at old ages, where active engagement in mental, physical, and social activities may postpone the onset of dementia, possibly by increasing the cognitive reserve (Mangialasche et al., 2012).

Despite growing evidence that simple lifestyle factors can improve our chances of developing dementia, the general public are unaware of this and could be increasing their risk (Yeo et al., 2007; Deckers et al., 2018; Heger et al., 2019). Lack of dementia prevention awareness is even more prominent in minority communities across the world (Uppal et al., 2014; Woo, 2017).

It is clear from the above that there is a unique opportunity for design research to employ visual communication and information communication design strategies to develop public health awareness campaigns. Furthermore, digital and product designers can engage the public through digital and physical interactive artefacts in developing an understanding of the risk factors and how different lifestyle choices can affect their health in later years.

As such, the focus in dementia diagnosis should shift from improving early diagnosis to improving mid-life prevention (O'Donnell et al., 2015). Again, this is an area where design research could contribute significantly and even lead the field, by focusing research especially in major life events of people in their 40s, 50s and 60s, such as having family, career change, retirement, etc. Research that addresses the impacts of such events in people's lives and health, by understanding how these risk factors are embedded in our lives and designing out the barriers healthier life styles in mid-life.

Within this context it is equally important to study the very much unexplored area of gender and dementia (Azad et al., 2007; Rocca et al., 2014; Bartlett et al., 2018). Addressing the lacuna in the literature in this, will help develop a better understanding of social, economic, cultural factors that increase the incidence of dementia amongst women in relation to physiological risk factors. Here design research will need to collaborate with other disciplines in humanities, such as gender studies and social and health sciences along with medical research.

Conclusion

Looking into the future, it is probable that dementia care and studies will begin to intersect more closely with a focus on everyday life. The study of the everyday has a relatively long history and whilst social theorists will differ in their understandings and constructions, essentially the study of everyday life is 'related to all activities' which have 'a common ground' (Lefebvre,

1991, p. 97). More recently, Scott (2009) has broken-down everyday life into three key dimensions: (i) social order; (ii) rituals and routines; and (iii) the taken-for-granted. Scott (2009) goes on to suggest that the most ordinary everyday life components are emotions, home, time, eating, health, shopping and leisure. Everyday life is also seen to be mundane with repeated cycles of human behaviour and actions that act to give us all a sense of security and familiarity. In many ways, living with a diagnosis dementia challenges and disrupts the routine and mundane patterns of everyday life, such as finding difficulty in social interactions and remembering, understanding the value of money, misidentifying close and loved relatives, becoming unable to tell the time and being and becoming lost in what is seemingly familiar surroundings. This is not a complete picture but it gives an idea about the direction of travel and how everyday life is affected on a minute by minute basis. Perhaps part of the future of design researchers and their evolving methods is to attune themselves more closely to the everyday and start to co-construct design solutions that create stability and activity in the lives of people living with dementia. There are many ways to do this, including attention on everyday technologies and in the everyday environments in which people with dementia live and interact. Arguably, the ten case studies in Part 2 of this book are attending to this everyday life agenda but without articulating it as such in the description of their work. Making this invisible link visible may well help to give a shape and structure to future design research work and its intersections with other disciplines and activities.

Linked closely to the above, it is also noticeable that design researchers are focussed on 'in the moment' work. For example, this focus was found in: the innovation that went into the development of Compassionate Design (Treadaway, 2018; and as seen in case study 8); the materials and objects that enabled people living with dementia to be present with the lived-again memories (such as those found in the availability of favourite playlists; and as seen in case study 7); and the importance of developing live music that drew on the co-creativity of people living with dementia and the immersion in such experiences (as seen in case study 10). Recently, Keady and his colleagues (2020) have developed a new conceptual framework for dementia studies that looks closely at the in the moment experiences and these authors have suggested that this is part of a cyclical continuum of moments that go through the steps of: creating the moment; being in the moment; ending the moment; and reliving the moment. If this analysis holds sway, then part of a future challenge for design researchers is to find ways to not only create moments for people living with dementia, but to keep people in the moment for longer, especially if that moment is seen as being a pleasurable and life-enhancing activity. Measuring the meaning of moments through such a positive lens and culture may also be helpful in future design research studies that involve people living with dementia, especially in the co-creative nature of the act. Moreover, evaluation of such moments could be measured in fractions of clock time if that is what is important, or possible, for people living with dementia and has made a difference to personal well-being. This positioning was seen repeatedly during the ten case studies in Part 2 of the book and a new conceptual lens wrapped around moments and everyday life might be a suitable signpost for future design research studies and methods.

In closing, this book has shown that dementia research cannot be addressed by the medical paradigm alone. It has revealed that as future research will focus on the everyday living experiences of people living with dementia, design research has the propensity to contribute significantly to it and lead research in this field. Nevertheless, if design research is to lead dementia research, design researchers would require more interdisciplinary training and evidence-based design to be able to address dementia in a holistic way and to contribute to the development of more person-centred future policies.

References

Azad, N. A., Al Bugami, M. and Loy-English, I. (2007). Gender differences in dementia risk factors. *Gender Medicine*, 4 (2): 120–129.

Bartlett, R., Gjernes, T., Lotherington, A. T. and Obstefelder, A. (2018). Gender, citizenship and dementia care: a scoping review of studies to inform policy and future research. *Health & Social Care in the Community*, 26 (1): 14–26.

Branco, R. M., Quental, J. and Ribeiro, Ó. (2017). Personalised participation: an approach to involve people with dementia and their families in a participatory design project. *CoDesign*, 13 (2): 127–143.

Brodaty, H. and Donkin, M. (2009). Family caregivers of people with dementia. *Dialogues in Clinical Neuroscience*, 11 (2): 217.

Calvert, L., Keady, J., Khetani, B., Riley, C., Open Doors Research Group and Swarbrick, C. (2020). '… this is my home and my neighbourhood with my very good and not so good memories': the story of autobiographical place-making and a recent life with dementia. *Dementia: The International Journal of Social Research and Practice*, 19 (1): 111–128.

Casale, M. A., Flicker, S. and Nixon, S. A. (2011). Fieldwork challenges: lessons learned from a North–South public health research partnership. *Health Promotion Practice*, 12 (5): 734–743.

Chaudhury, H. and Cooke, H. (2014). Design matters in dementia care: the role of the physical environment in dementia care settings. *Excellence in Dementia Care*, 2: 144–158.

Cheema, A. R., Mehmood, A. and Khan, F. A. (2018). Challenges of research in rural poverty: lessons from large field surveys. *Development in Practice*, 28 (5): 714–719.

Chen, S., Boyle, L. L., Conwell, Y., Xiao, S. and Chiu, H. F. K. (2014). The challenges of dementia care in rural China. *International Psychogeriatrics*, 26 (7): 1059–1064.

Daly Lynn, J., Rondón-Sulbarán, J., Quinn, E., Ryan, A., McCormack, B. and Martin, S. (2019). A systematic review of electronic assistive technology within supporting living environments for people with dementia. *Dementia*, 18 (7–8): 2371–2435.

Deckers, K., van Boxtel, M. P., Schiepers, O. J., de Vugt, M., Munoz Sanchez, J. L., Anstey, K. J., Brayne, C., Dartigues, J.-F., Engedal, K., Kivipelto, M., Ritchie, K., Starr, J. M., Yaffe, K., Irving, K., Verhey, F. R. J. and Sebastian Köhler, S. (2015). Target risk factors for dementia prevention: a systematic review and Delphi consensus study on the evidence from observational studies. *International Journal of Geriatric Psychiatry*, 30 (3): 234–246.

Deckers, K., Köhler, S., van Boxtel, M., Verhey, F., Brayne, C. and Fleming, J. (2018). Lack of associations between modifiable risk factors and dementia in the very old: findings from the Cambridge City over-75s cohort study. *Aging & Mental Health*, 22 (10): 1272–1278.

Durand-Morat, A., Wailes, E. J. and Nayga Jr, R. M. (2015). Challenges of conducting contingent valuation studies in developing countries. *American Journal of Agricultural Economics*, 98 (2): 597–609.

Ferri, C. P. and Jacob, K. S. (2017). Dementia in low-income and middle-income countries: different realities mandate tailored solutions. *PLoS Medicine*, 14 (3): e1002271.

Førsund, L. H., Grov, E. K., Helvik, A. S., Juvet, L. K., Skovdahl, K. and Eriksen, S. (2018). The experience of lived space in persons with dementia: a systematic meta-synthesis. *BMC Geriatrics*, 18 (1): 33.

Godoy-Ruiz, P., Cole, D. C., Lenters, L. and McKenzie, K. (2016). Developing collaborative approaches to international research: perspectives of new global health researchers. *Global Public Health*, 11 (3): 253–275.

Gowans, G., Dye, R., Alm, N., Vaughan, P., Astell, A. and Ellis, M. (2007). Designing the interface between dementia patients, caregivers and computer-based intervention. *The Design Journal*, 10 (1): 12–23.

Gray, K., Evans, S. C., Griffiths, A. and Schneider, J. (2017). Critical reflections on methodological challenge in arts and dementia evaluation and research. *Dementia*, 1471301217734478.

Heger, I., Deckers, K., van Boxtel, M., de Vugt, M., Hajema, K., Verhey, F. and Köhler, S. (2019). Dementia awareness and risk perception in middle-aged and older individuals: baseline results of the MijnBreincoach survey on the association between lifestyle and brain health. *BMC Public Health*, 19 (1): 1–9.

Hendriks, N., Huybrechts, L., Wilkinson, A. and Slegers, K. (2014). "Challenges in doing participatory design with people with dementia." In *Proceedings of the 13th Participatory Design Conference: Short Papers, Industry Cases, Workshop Descriptions, Doctoral Consortium papers, and Keynote Abstracts-Volume 2*, pp. 33–36. New York: Association for Computing Machinery.

Hendriks, N., Slegers, K. and Duysburgh, P. (2015). Codesign with people living with cognitive or sensory impairments: a case for method stories and uniqueness. *CoDesign*, 11 (1): 70–82.

Hendriks, N., Truyen, F. and Duval, E. (2013). "Designing with Dementia: Guidelines for Participatory Design Together with Persons with Sementia." In *IFIP Conference on Human-Computer Interaction*, pp. 649–666. Berlin, Heidelberg: Springer.

Herholz, S. C., Herholz, R. S. and Herholz, K. (2013). Non-pharmacological interventions and neuroplasticity in early stage Alzheimer's disease. *Expert Review of Neurotherapeutics*, 13 (11): 1235–1245.

Hubbard, G., Downs, M. G. and Tester, S. (2003). Including older people with dementia in research: challenges and strategies. *Aging & Mental Health*, 7 (5): 351–362.

Iltanen-Tähkävuori, S., Wikberg, M. and Topo, P. (2012). Design and dementia: a case of garments designed to prevent undressing. *Dementia*, 11 (1): 49–59.

Jakob, A. and Collier, L. (2017). Sensory enrichment for people living with dementia: increasing the benefits of multisensory environments in dementia care through design. *Design for Health*, 1 (1): 115–133.

Johannessen, A. and Möller, A. (2013). Experiences of persons with early-onset dementia in everyday life: a qualitative study. *Dementia*, 12 (4): 410–424.

Johnston, K., Preston, R., Strivens, E., Qaloewai, S. and Larkins, S. (2019). Understandings of dementia in low and middle income countries and amongst indigenous peoples: a systematic review and qualitative meta-synthesis. *Aging & Mental Health*, 24 (8): 1–13.

Jones, D. (2015). A family living with Alzheimer's disease: the communicative challenges. *Dementia*, 14 (5): 555–573.

Keady, J., Campbell, S., Clark, A., Dowlen, R., Elvish, R., Jones, L., Kindell, J., Swarbrick, S. and Williams, S. (2020; accepted for publication). Re-thinking and re-positioning 'being in the moment' within a continuum of moments: introducing a new conceptual framework for dementia studies. *Ageing & Society*, accepted July 2020, 1–22. doi:10.1017/S0144686X20001014

Kenning, G. and Treadaway, C. (2018). Designing for dementia: iterative grief and transitional objects. *Design Issues*, 34 (1): 42–53.

Lages, C. R., Pfajfar, G. and Shoham, A. (2015). Challenges in conducting and publishing research on the Middle East and Africa in leading journals. *International Marketing Review*, 32 (1): 52–77.

Lefebvre, H. (1991). *Critique of Everyday Life:* Volume 1, John Moore trans., London: Verso.

Livingston, G., Sommerlad, A., Orgeta, V., Costafreda, S. G., Huntley, J., Ames, D., Ballard, C., Banerjee, S., Burns, A., Cohen-Mansfield, J., Cooper, C., Fox, N., Gitlin, L. N., Howard, R., Kales, H. C., Larson, E. B., Ritchie, K., Rockwood, K., Sampson, E. L., Samus, Q., Schneider, L. S., Selbæk, G., Teri, L. and Mukadam, N. (2017). Dementia prevention, intervention, and care. *The Lancet*, 390 (10113): 2673–2734.

Maestre, G. E. (2012). Assessing dementia in resource-poor regions. *Current Neurology and Neuroscience Reports*, 12 (5): 511–519.

Mangialasche, F., Kivipelto, M., Solomon, A. and Fratiglioni, L. (2012). Dementia prevention: current epidemiological evidence and future perspective. *Alzheimer's Research & Therapy*, 4 (1): 6.

McKeown, J., Clarke, A., Ingleton, C. and Repper, J. (2010). Actively involving people with dementia in qualitative research. *Journal of Clinical Nursing*, 19 (13–14): 1935–1943.

Moore, T. F. and Hollett, J. (2003). Giving voice to persons living with dementia: the researcher's opportunities and challenges. *Nursing Science Quarterly*, 16 (2): 163–167.

Morrissey, K., Wood, G., Green, D., Pantidi, N. and McCarthy, J. (2016). "'I'm a Rambler, I'm a Gambler, I'm a Long Way from Home' The Place of Props, Music, and Design in Dementia Care." In *Proceedings of the 2016 ACM Conference on Designing Interactive Systems*, pp. 1008–1020.

Moyle, W. and Murfield, J. E. (2013). Health-related quality of life in older people with severe dementia: challenges for measurement and management. *Expert Review of Pharmacoeconomics & Outcomes Research*, 13 (1): 109–122.

Murko, P. and Kunze, C. (2015). "Tangible Memories: Exploring the Use of Tangible Interfaces for Occupational Therapy in Dementia Care." In *Proceedings of the 3rd European Conference on Design4Health* (Vol. 13, p. 16).

Norton, S., Matthews, F. E., Barnes, D. E., Yaffe, K. and Brayne, C., (2014). Potential for primary prevention of Alzheimer's disease: an analysis of population-based data. *The Lancet Neurology*, 13 (8): 788–794;

O'Donnell, C. A., Manera, V., Köhler, S. and Irving, K., (2015). Promoting modifiable risk factors for dementia: is there a role for general practice? *British Journal of General Practice*, 65 (640): 567–568.

Pasluosta, C. F., Gassner, H., Winkler, J., Klucken, J. and Eskofier, B. M. (2015). An emerging era in the management of Parkinson's disease: wearable technologies and the internet of things. *IEEE Journal of Biomedical and Health Informatics*, 19 (6): 1873–1881.

Prince, M., Acosta, D., Albanese, E., Arizaga, R., Ferri, C. P., Guerra, M., Huang, Y., Jacob, K. S., Jimenez-Velazquez, I. Z., Rodriguez, J. L., Salas, A., Luisa Sosa, A., Sousa, R., Uwakwe, R., van der Poel, R., Williams, J. and Wortmann, M. (2008). Ageing and dementia in low and middle income countries–Using research to engage with public and policy makers. *International Review of Psychiatry*, 20 (4): 332–343.

Prince, M., Comas-Herrera, A., Knapp, M., Guerchet, M. and Karagiannidou, M. (2016). World Alzheimer report 2016: improving healthcare for people living with dementia: coverage, quality and costs now and in the future. Alzheimer's Disease International (ADI), London, UK.

Rocca, W. A., Mielke, M. M., Vemuri, P. and Miller, V. M. (2014). Sex and gender differences in the causes of dementia: a narrative review. *Maturitas*, 79 (2): 196–201.

Rodgers, P. A. (2018). Co-designing with people living with dementia. *CoDesign*, 14 (3): 188–202.

Sanders, E. B. N. and Stappers, P. J. (2008). Co-creation and the new landscapes of design. *Co-Design*, 4(1): 5–18.

Scott, S. (2009). *Making Sense of Everyday Life*. London: Polity.

Semrau, M., Evans-Lacko, S., Koschorke, M., Ashenafi, L. and Thornicroft, G. (2015). Stigma and discrimination related to mental illness in low-and middle-income countries. *Epidemiology and Psychiatric Sciences*, 24 (5): 382–394.

Shoemaker, L. K., Kazley, A. S. and White, A. (2010). Making the case for evidence-based design in healthcare: a descriptive case study of organizational decision making. *HERD: Health Environments Research & Design Journal*, 4 (1): 56–88.

Soilemezi, D., Drahota, A., Crossland, J., Stores, R. and Costall, A. (2017). Exploring the meaning of home for family caregivers of people with dementia. *Journal of Environmental Psychology*, 51: 70–81.

Subramaniam, P. and Woods, B. (2010). Towards the therapeutic use of information and communication technology in reminiscence work for people with dementia: a systematic review. *International Journal of Computers in Healthcare*, 1 (2): 106–125.

Treadaway, C. (2018). Compassionate Design: How to design for advanced dementia. A toolkit for designers. Pub. Cardiff Metropolitan University, ISBN 978-0-9929482-8-3

Tsekleves, E., Bingley, A. F., Luján Escalante, M. A. and Gradinar, A. (2020). Engaging people with dementia in designing playful and creative practices: co-design or co-creation?. *Dementia*, 19 (3): 915–931.

Ulrich, R. S., Zimring, C., Zhu, X., DuBose, J., Seo, H. B., Choi, Y. S., Quan, X. and Joseph, A. (2008). A review of the research literature on evidence-based healthcare design. *HERD: Health Environments Research & Design Journal*, 1 (3): 61–125.

Uppal, G. K., Bonas, S. and Philpott, H. (2014). Understanding and awareness of dementia in the Sikh community. *Mental Health, Religion & Culture*, 17 (4): 400–414.

Van Hoof, J., Rutten, P. G., Struck, C., Huisman, E. R. and Kort, H. S. (2015). The integrated and evidence-based design of healthcare environments. *Architectural Engineering and Design Management*, 11 (4): 243–263.

Vance, D. E., Roberson, A. J., McGuinness, T. M. and Fazeli, P. L. (2010). How neuroplasticity and cognitive reserve protect cognitive functioning. *Journal of Psychosocial Nursing and Mental Health Services*, 48 (4): 23–30.

Visser, F. S., Stappers, P. J., Van der Lugt, R. and Sanders, E. B. (2005). Contextmapping: experiences from practice. *CoDesign*, 1 (2): 119–149.

Wang, Q., Markopoulos, P., Yu, B., Chen, W. and Timmermans, A. (2017). Interactive wearable systems for upper body rehabilitation: a systematic review. *Journal of Neuroengineering and Rehabilitation*, 14 (1): 20.

Wang, J., Xiao, L. D., He, G. P. and De Bellis, A. (2014). Family caregiver challenges in dementia care in a country with undeveloped dementia services. *Journal of Advanced Nursing*, 70 (6): 1369–1380.

White, S. and Pettit, J. (2007). "Participatory Approaches and the Measurement of Human Well-being." In McGillivray, M. (ed) *Human Well-Being*, pp. 240–267. New York: Palgrave Macmillan.

Woo, B. K. (2017). Dementia health promotion for Chinese Americans. *Cureus*, 9 (6): 1–40.

Wortmann, M. (2012). Dementia: a global health priority-highlights from an ADI and World Health Organization report. *Alzheimer's Research & Therapy*, 4 (5): 40.

Xia, F., Yang, L. T., Wang, L. and Vinel, A. (2012). Internet of things. *International Journal of Communication Systems*, 25 (9): 1101.

Yeo, L. J., Horan, M. A., Jones, M. and Pendleton, N. (2007). Perceptions of risk and prevention of dementia in the healthy elderly. *Dementia and Geriatric Cognitive Disorders*, 23 (6): 368–371.

Zimring, C. and Bosch, S. (2008). Building the evidence base for evidence-based design. *Environment and Behavior*, 40: 147–150

Index

Printed in the United States
by Baker & Taylor Publisher Services